BUILDING UP A NEW WORLD

BUILDING UP
A NEW WORLD

Congregational
Organizing for
Transformative Impact

Edited by Anne Dunlap and Vahisha Hasan

Love & Liberation —

Blessings
of Wellness
Vahisha
Hasan

the pilgrim press

The Pilgrim Press, 1300 East 9th Street
Cleveland, Ohio 44114
thepilgrimpress.com

Published 2023.

Scripture quotations, unless otherwise noted, are from the New Revised Standard Version of the Bible, © 1989 by the Division of Christian Education of the National Council of Churches of Christ in the United States of America. Used by permission. Changes have been made for inclusivity.

"We Are Building Up a New World," music in the public domain ("We Are Climbing Jacob's Ladder"), lyrics by Vincent Harding. Used with permission of Rachel Harding and Jonathan Harding.

Printed on acid-free paper.

Library of Congress Cataloging-in-Publication Data on file.
LCCN: 2022951468

ISBN 978-0-8298-0042-5 (alk. paper)
ISBN 978-0-8298-0043-2 (ebook)

Printed in The United States of America.

DEDICATION and GRATITUDE

. . .

Dedicated to all our heartbeats.
Yours.
Ours.

The heartbeats of our ancestors.
The heartbeats of our children's grandchildren's children.
The heartbeats of air, fire, water, earth,
the sun, moon, sky, stars,
the creatures, plants, trees, and spirit.
The heartbeats of every freedom fighter,
movement worker, artist, teacher, healer,
who shaped us for this moment.

And to the Divine heartbeat,
Pulsing life into the universe,
Pulsing justice,
Pulsing liberation,
Pulsing love.

With deepest gratitude to all our beloveds who held us, nourished us,
encouraged us, challenged us, and fed us, as we worked on this project.
To each contributor who brought so much love
and commitment to their chapter.
And to each other, for the gift of being and working on this together.

CONTENTS

. . .

. . .

FOREWORD

. . .

Building Up a New World: Congregational Organizing for Transformative Impact is an invitation to reimagine faith-rooted organizing from culturally diverse perspectives. The community of writers are on-the-ground witnesses to racism, colonialism, terrorism, acts of violence, physical assaults, state sanctioned violence, and militarism.

The contributors are curators and storytellers who share their personal experiences organizing and making what the late civil rights leader and US Congressman John Lewis spoke of as Good Trouble.[1] My work as a racial justice advocate and antiracism educator has been strengthened by these wise justice warriors as they honor their ancestors and put their bodies on the frontlines of faith rooted in love.

Each chapter provides relevant guidance with countercultural tools, resources, and practical steps for implementing actions leading towards incorporating cultural organizing skills. Faith seeking justice means every member—in every region of the country, in every city, rural community, and small town—can become a frontline radical organizer for justice.

The contributors are wise truth-seekers and truth-tellers, local pastors and lay leaders, talented lyricists, musicians, and poets. Some have deep roots nurtured in rural communities and congregations. Others have urban insights, while another writer has an Indigenous birthright to land stolen by settler colonialists. They come to this work with cultural organizing skills. These people represent the collective spirit and spectrum of God's family as described in Revelation 7:9, "from every nation, from all tribes and peoples and languages."

The land we live on, of all fifty states, belongs to Indigenous peoples. It was not discovered but stolen from its original inhabitants. Our nation misrepresents itself as belonging to European settlers who created race categories to justify myths that named them as superior to other peoples. Their ideology of white supremacy emboldened them to steal native people's land and enslave African-descended people for over 250 years. The Christian church sanctioned colonialism, enslavement, genocide, ethnic cleansing, and theft of lands and resources, which resulted in global death sentences for Indigenous and African peoples. The names of the many people who stewarded the land for over 10,000 years are not acknowledged and honored as sacred landowners. They are the Hopi, Powhatan, Cherokee, Pequot, Mohican, Lakota, Cheyenne, Crow, Cree, Haudenosaunee, Anishinaabe, and many more. These sacred people have organized and continue to organize to fight their oppressors.

It is then important to name that community organizing did not begin with Saul Alinsky. In the United States, righteous resistance and organizing methodologies fueled revolts by enslaved people and indigenous self-defense in the 1600s. Resistance and protest remain a current reality into the twenty-first century. Models of community organizing are methods used by groups of people to protect themselves from oppression, from invasion by nation-states, and from imperial occupation in the form of dehumanizing policies and imprisonment. Community organizing models inspire radical resistance and can even be found in various books in the Hebrew Bible. Organizing is a liberation strategy used to resist white supremacy and state-sanctioned violence as witnessed during the ongoing murders of people of color, which ignited a global uprising after the murder of George Floyd in 2020. Today's community organizing is a continuation of resistance movements, protests, and revolts addressing injustices around the globe.

I am honored to walk alongside such a powerful community of strong solidarity partners who lift diverse practices and traditions that represent a radical faith. Some of the contributors follow a Middle-Eastern Jewish theologian and teacher who masterfully organized his community, liberated colonized minds, breathed new life into oppressed rural communities, and often empowered women when met with restrictive heterosexism and misogyny. The writers are deeply committed to bringing about justice for all through community organizing strategies based on their lived experiences and personal investment in the sacred. Each of the writers believe in liberation for all and work towards resisting imperial evil posing as a government entity in the twenty-first century.

Injustices continue to permeate the Christian church and society, dominating people's thinking based on historical and contemporary ideologies of inhumane behaviors towards people of African, Native, Asian and Pacific Islander, and Latin descents. Injustices are a result of human behaviors influenced by deeply held beliefs that there are groups of human beings who are disposable, inferior, and expendable.

"The master's tools will never dismantle the master's house. They may allow us to temporarily beat him at his own game, but they will never enable us to bring about genuine change."

—Audre Lorde[2]

Structural tools are developed by those of white wealth to codify their self-serving empire building. They employ others who believe and think like them to write statements, edicts, laws, constitutions, doctrines, and policies claiming exclusive rights to inherit the world, including its abundance of resources, by any means necessary.

Lethal weapons are used to control, enslave, ethnically cleanse, and annihilate the oppressed when they act for freedom and liberation by engaging in uprisings, resistance movements, revolts, and protest to government sanctions against black and brown bodies. This historical context sets the stage for communities organizing against white supremacy, state sanctioned violence, and individual acts of physical threats and violence.

Supporters of racism, militarism, and domestic terrorism disagree and cringe at the use of the words *white supremacy*. However, settler colonialism is a pandemic that continues to impact communities of color. Within the pages of this timely book are bold thought leaders, clergy, activists, and community organizers who use their voices to unashamedly encourage people to speak up, rise up, and intervene at every level within their cities, states, and rural communities for justice.

Some of the stories provide insights into radical organizing and counterprotest strategies enacted in the name of defending the rights and freedoms of black and brown bodies from white nationalists and supremacists on the streets of Charlottesville, VA on August 12, 2017.

For those who want to better understand their role in creating a just world for all, this is a resource that will strengthen your journey towards becoming a well-trained community organizer. This collection of writings is a call to action and an offering of applicable tools for the journey. Upon completing the book, you will no longer sit on the sidelines, watching and listening to rhetoric tearing our nation apart by those who prioritize profits over people.

The call is to lean into the lives and learnings, and then implement the community organizing tools and resources necessary for the liberation of humanity.

And finally, this book demands readers to expand their peripheral vision to see what God sees: humanity in non-binary, non-restrictive gender identities and orientations with a conviction to live life beyond traditionalisms that bind, kill, destroy, cage, incarcerate, poison, deprive, enslave, ethnically cleanse, grab land, and constrict one's beliefs and daily practices. The invitation has been extended and new tools for strategies of justice are waiting for you.

Rev. Dr. Velda Love
UCC Minister for Racial Justice
Justice and Local Church Ministries

Notes

1. John Lewis: *Good Trouble*, dir. Dawn Porter (2021; New York: Magnolia Pictures), https://www.johnlewisgoodtrouble.com/.
2. Audre Lorde, "The Master's Tools Will Never Dismantle the Master's House," in *Sister Outsider: Essays and Speeches* (New York: The Crossing Press Feminist Series, 1984), 112.

. . .

INTRODUCTION
The Building of This Book

. . .

We are building up a new world,
Builders must be strong.[1]

ORGANIZING FOUNDATIONS: AN ORIGIN STORY

In another lifetime, formerly known as November 2019, we, Anne Dunlap and Vahisha Hasan, were invited by the United Church of Christ to curate and co-edit a book that would provide tools for congregational organizing. We were both honored and excited about this opportunity. To be clear, we were excited because we love each other, and we appreciate any excuse to sojourn together. And because, in a time of rising white Christian supremacist violence and ever-deeper investment in oppressive structures by white — most often Christian — power and wealth, this project offered an opportunity to move the Christian masses towards a different vision, to call people of the pews to put their faith into action.

In our experience and assessment of the church we, as long-time organizers, have observed that *the church is often good at advocacy, but not actually good at organizing to build power or to change structures and systems, including our own denominations.* We will do a

· 1 ·

voter registration drive but won't challenge legislation stripping people of voter rights; we will hold a charity drive but won't address systems that cause perpetual need; we will do book studies and have committee hearings on issue after issue, but not make the needed structural changes that create the conditions for justice; we will hang up a Black Lives Matter banner but won't consider abolition or giving to national bailout funds; we will choose not to "rock the boat" rather than challenge congregations to do transformative organizing work. *This transformative shift to organizing towards collective transformation of systems that historically oppress is within us as individuals and communities.*

Please note, *by church we mean people in the pews*, not just the preaching or "recognized" leading people. We want pew people to locate yourselves in this book and *see yourselves as capable agents of change* already within a powerbase that can be a part of impactful social change. So many of our faith rooted organizing experiences are only about organizing the pastor and leadership. Which is important, and also insufficient, if the people they lead only move at the leaders' event/campaign-based prompting and not from the depths of the pew people's own call to the rich discipleship of generative social change. Church hierarchy can be fruitful, but it is also often stifling, as is the complicated nature of hierarchies.

Anyhoohow (Vahisha's mother's language), we began working in January 2020, living in shared docs and spreadsheets and dreaming and scheming with our other favorite human, Rev. Tracy Howe. We began by framing our content addressing our assessment above and asking the questions: *what are the tools, skills, and practices congregations need to move like organizers?* We began sketching out chapters that would offer structural analysis and organizing frameworks for congregations and discussing the organizing practices and models we wanted to focus on. We began identifying the super dope folks we knew who were actively organizing across a broad spectrum of how faith shows up in the world. We were grateful and humbled by the responses from amazing organizers who saw the potential good of our shared effort, and many emails, Zooms, and contracts later, we had the beginning outline of an amazing book filled with amazing places of learning from beyond-amazing contributors.

Then COVID. (March 11, 2020)
Then Ahmaud Arbery. (February 23, 2020)
Then Breonna Taylor. (March 13, 2020)
Then George Floyd. (May 25, 2020)
Then the Summer of Uprisings for Black Life. (Summer 2020)
Then the US Presidential election (November 3, 2020)
Then the January Insurrection (January 6, 2021)
And then vaccines.
And then variants.
And then...
And then...

Our lives forever changed.

COVID became the overarching theme of, well, everything.

These Black lives became the name and face of the ongoing rallying cry of Black Lives Matter!

Globally it felt like the world erupted. Over and over again. This new global context impacted everything about this book. Every person with any level of involvement in this book was actively involved in trying to survive COVID, mourning beloveds who didn't, and protesting, resisting, advocating, and organizing around the mattering of these particular and all Black lives.

We name this context, this origin story, because this book was not born in a vacuum, and indeed organizing does not happen in a vacuum. Organizing, and this book offering congregational tools for organizing, are responses to material conditions that impact our lives, our loves, our breath, our bodies. And we used the organizing skills we have, and that we were learning from our contributors, to build this book in this historical moment.

CRUCIAL BUILDING PRACTICES: HOW WE BUILT THIS BOOK

We, Anne and Vahisha, are organizers with seventy years combined— and counting!—of organizing experience towards racial justice, economic justice, immigration, LGBTQ liberation, indigenous self-determination, abolition of police, prisons, and the death penalty . . . the list goes on. In faith spaces and beyond faith spaces. In the streets, in the halls of power, in our classrooms, from our pulpits, around kitchen tables. Through political education, healing work, campaigns, direct actions, and more.

Our friendship began in January 2017, when Anne was in Vahisha's hometown, Charlotte, North Carolina, representing Showing Up for Racial Justice (SURJ) with United Methodist Women to protest the horrible anti-trans House Bill 2—the infamous "bathroom bill" that Vahisha was organizing against. The first time we met in person during that trip was actually in the Charlotte Douglas Airport, when we protested the Muslim travel ban together (and almost got arrested), right after THE inauguration. We connected deeply over those days and began finding ways to work together. Anne invited Vahisha to co-facilitate a campaign of SURJ-Faith, which Anne coordinates, to equip and support congregations to divest from policing. Anne accepted the invitation to write devotionals for Vahisha's three-volume series, *Resipiscence: A Lenten Devotional for Dismantling White Supremacy*, co-edited by Nichola Torbett, one of the contributors to this current book. Then we again conspired for positive social change together, beginning in the summer of 2019, as ongoing cohort members of Vanderbilt Divinity School's Public Theology and Racial Justice Collaborative.

Having this depth of friendship, camaraderie, and organizing experience together was invaluable not only because *relationships are crucial in organizing*, but also because we became a pastoral team that was now shepherding the contributors of the book—and ourselves!—in the context of global crisis. We held so much space for pastoral care of each other and our writers because individually and collectively we were all navigating the absolute most. The most being and including a global response to the pandemic, an exponential rise in anti-Asian and antisemitic hate crimes, a ramping up of targeting immigrants and asylum seekers, the brutal murdering of Black life, attacks on trans beloveds, and ongoing state violence against Indigenous land and water protectors. People in our lives were dying, and losing their jobs, and housing insecure, and not necessarily safe at home. Others didn't have the access to resources they needed for a virtual world fully in quarantine. Our mental and physical health suffered. We couldn't get to our loved ones and were confronted with the need to adjust our lives in previously unimaginable ways. All while we fought on the systemic battlefields of classism, racism, xenophobia, ableism, homophobia, and interpersonal conflicts created by people just being plain awful in their fear and scarcity of mindset, action, and inaction.

This shepherding became part of the ethos you will find in this book: *How do we hold each other while we do this challenging work? How do we face the challenges within our own lives and bodies while we face the challenges in our communities?* Every Thursday for over two years, Anne, Vahisha, and often Tracy, met for an hour or more. We thought we were just going to strategize editing and publishing, and while that did happen, we also prayed and cried and laughed our way through two years of personal, global, pandemic, and political rollercoasters of ups and downs. We discovered we needed to "crip the timeline" multiple times, for our writers and for us—learning from our chapter how to center disability justice and healing and wellness in ways we truly needed to pause and process and honor. Vahisha was typically in pajamas and often horizontal. Anne's partner and cat made many encouraging appearances. And Tracy often showed up with the most remarkable child and a picturesque backdrop that helped us breathe through all of the things. *This is how we made it through together, and how we pray you all make it through, how we all make it through, together.*

As you can tell, nothing about this curating and editing process went quite as we thought it would. Nevertheless, we did come through to the other side and are proud of what is offered here. We're proud of how intentional we were about choosing contributors who have lived, deep organizing experience in the areas we asked them to write about. We're proud of how we're offering tools to congregations that some might consider pretty radical, but that address necessary work for getting us free from oppression. We're proud of taking the time to get our biblical power analysis right by addressing antisemitic biblical interpretation in the editing process—that could've almost become a whole other book! And we're proud of how we centered our contributors' voices and experiences; we were surprised at how consistently we needed to invite people into liberating their voices and telling their stories and to remind them that their voices and stories mattered, framed by their wisdom and life experiences. This makes us wonder how many people sitting in congregations are not lifting their voices because somewhere along the way they were sent messages telling them that what they experienced and had to say were not valuable and sacred. It was a joy to experience these contributors as they experienced validation and support, and we have been intentional about allowing the voices of these contributors to shine through. *We find joy in hoping this same valuing of life and voice can come forth as congregations shift to organizing as much or more than they are programming.*

BUILDING UP: THE TOOLBOX

Our book revolves around three subject areas: *Organizing Foundations* offers chapters on structural analysis and key organizing building blocks. *Crucial Building Practices* are guiding practices we want you to center and include no matter what form your organizing takes. And in *Building Up: Putting It All Together*, you will find a set of "blueprints" for what your organizing can look like that are crucial to collective liberation and protecting our communities in this time of rising violence, and that are translatable to a variety of contexts. For example, our chapter on mutual aid comes out of immigrant experiences, but could be used to build mutual aid projects such as abortion funds or healthcare access for trans kids.

Finally, in this book, you will notice a theme that comes up consistently:

YOU ARE ALREADY ORGANIZERS.

Currently, you may only be organizing programmatic aspects of church. What would it look like to transfer those skills to organizing for transformative social change? You already know how to power map because you know exactly who to go to in order to get what you want done or not done. You know how to phone-tree to make sure folks show up to church programs, wear the designated colors or uniform, and bring whatever food or decorations or props are necessary for a successful program. You clearly know how to raise money, and you know how to run the pastor/leadership off when they are not in alignment with the direction of the church body. What we and the contributors are asking, encouraging, and demonstrating is how to *shift those transferable organizational skills to build systemic change in a world full of people who need the church to meaningfully Organize Organize Organize!*

* * *

BUILDING UP A NEW WORLD

Courage, people, don't get weary,
Though the way be long.[2]

Dr. Vincent Harding was a brilliant and deep-hearted Black historian and freedom movement leader.[3] Dr. Harding was a mentor to many, including Anne. In space after space, Dr. Harding offered a simple song he created to help us remember, in those hard times, what we are doing; to encourage us to keep going; and to remind us to stay grounded in the sacred.

The title of this book honors and reflects the urging of the song to do our part in transforming the world towards one more full of justice, compassion, love, and freedom. The song was often in Anne's mind as we worked on this book: if we want congregations to be contributing to building a new world, what new (and old) tools, skills, and knowledge do they, do we, need?

What are we doing? We mean individually, and especially we mean collectively. *What are we doing when we organize?* What are we doing when we center disability justice? When we assure Indigenous self-determination? When we build mutual aid networks and put our bodies and reputations on the line and keep one another safe?

We are building up a new world. Not "we" because we're the only and oh so special ones; not "new" because we suddenly thought of it, as if the movement for justice and freedom hasn't been flowing for generation upon generation. No, we gathered here in this space together, joining our breath and our voices and our labor together to sing this freedom song; we the present ones, the ancestors, and the ones to come—we are wading into the river, wading deeper into the river that flows towards collective liberation—towards a new world that is new because we have found new ways of being human together, of relating to one another, the creatures, the land together, new ways that are often very old ways, recovered and re-mixed, drawing us deeper into the river, the river that, as Dr. Harding says,

> moves toward a freedom that liberates the whole person and humanizes the entire society, pressing us beyond the boundaries of race, class, and nationality . . . this is the magnificent opening toward which the river has been moving, the great ocean of humanity's best hope that it has always held and nurtured at the center of its own bursting life.[4]

We are building up a new world. Our most fervent prayer is that this book helps you and your congregation to deepen not only your organizing skills, but also your collective commitment to a beautiful, thriving, just, and compassionate new world.

We are building up a new world
We are building up a new world
We are building up a new world
Builders must be strong

Courage, sisters, don't get weary
Courage, brothers, don't get weary
Courage, people, don't get weary
Though the way be long.

Rise, shine, give God glory
Rise, shine, give God glory
Rise, shine, give God glory
Children of the light.[5]

Notes

1. Verse 1, "We Are Building Up a New World," music in the public domain ("We are Climbing Jacob's Ladder"), lyrics by Vincent Harding. Used with permission of Rachel Harding and Jonathan Harding.

2. Verse 2, "We Are Building Up a New World," music in the public domain ("We Are Climbing Jacob's Ladder"), lyrics by Vincent Harding. Used with permission of Rachel Harding and Jonathan Harding.

3. Learn more about Dr. Vincent Harding at The Veterans Hope Project, "Vincent Gordon Harding," https://www.veteransofhope.org/founders/vincent-gordon-harding/. Veterans of Hope is an organization founded by Dr. Harding and his wife Rosemarie Freeney Harding.

4. Dr. Vincent Harding, *There Is a River: The Black Struggle for Freedom in America* (New York: Harcourt, Brace, and Company, 1981), xxiv.

5. "We Are Building Up a New World."

SECTION I

. . .

Organizing Foundations

1

· · ·

WHITE SUPREMACY AND THE STRUCTURE OF OPPRESSION

· · ·

ANNE DUNLAP

REFLECTION

At sixteen, I knew I would dedicate my life to justice. God laid that call on my heart at the 1986 Presbyterian Youth Triennium (an every-three-year gathering) when a young adult spoke of her work with the Sanctuary Movement in Tucson, Arizona, and was followed by a Salvadoran refugee who had fled state repression and torture. Both shared about the United States' involvement in funding and training the Salvadoran government to crush peasant-led organizing against poor wages, land theft, and state violence.[1] My heart pounded. I wanted to live in a world where people did not have to live in that kind of fear. I wanted to be part of making that violence stop.

Ever since, for over thirty-five years, I've been part of movements working to build a better world. Over time, I learned that the US commitment to state violence in El Salvador was not an aberration, not a matter of changing a few policies, nor reforming a few practices. The entire US structure itself is inherently and intentionally violent and oppressive, and our bloody support of El Salvador was only one expression of that violence. As a white person, this truth was kept from me and has taken decades of unlearning—a process still ongoing.

I am immensely grateful to the Black feminist/womanist and Indigenous women activists-scholars I draw from here, and most especially all the Black, Indigenous, immigrant, QTPOC, and poor and working-class activists, organizers, and feminist, womanist, and liberation theologians in the United States, Mexico, and Central America who had patience with all my certainly fumbling questions over these decades. They continue teaching me that what we are facing is not a generally good or even benign set of institutions that just need reforms to function a little better for a few more people, but rather an entire edifice—an entire structure called white supremacy that is upheld by violent mechanisms and logics. The mechanisms are *how* the structure does what it does, and the logics are the reasons *why* the structure does what it does. These mechanisms and logics, the how and the why, run through every institution and indeed, every one of us. True liberation is dismantling that whole structure and building a new world of justice, collective care, accountability, and compassion.[2]

WHITE SUPREMACY AND THE STRUCTURE OF OPPRESSION

White Supremacy is an historically based, institutionally perpetuated system of exploitation and oppression of continents, nations, and peoples of color by white peoples and nations of the European continent, for the purpose of maintaining and defending a system of wealth, power, and privilege.

Betita Martinez, SNCC Organizer[3]

We are starting here because understanding this system, this structure—how it operates, who it benefits, how it makes meaning out of bodies and relationships—is crucial to our organizing. Without it, we miss much of what needs to be done and our organizing is thus not as effective as it could be. Without it, we do not understand that *this structure of oppression does not love us,* does not care about us, and so we labor under the impression that some reforms here and there that allow a few more people more access to success in this structure—that some changing of hearts and minds without changing power structures—will be sufficient to the task of collective liberation. So let us get clear about what this structure actually is in order to forge a grounding place for our organizing.

White supremacy is the structure of oppression in which the United States lives and moves and has its being and which we export around the world. White supremacy is not about interpersonal prejudices or individual acts of hate. White supremacy is about power—who has it, to what ends, and what meaning is made out of that power—and it is baked into every institution we move within: politics, education, health care, policing, you name it. Each of these interrelated institutions functions as Betita Martinez states above: "for the purpose of maintaining and defending a system of wealth, power, and privilege" to the benefit of a small minority of white people.

By every institution, yes, I mean even the church, as white supremacy is also a theological construction. Theology is essentially about meaning-making, and white supremacy makes meaning out of what it means to be human and who is the Divine. White supremacy makes meaning out of people's bodies—whose are worthy and pure and good and able (white), and whose are criminal, a threat, deserving of punishment, disposable (Black, Indigenous, immigrant, disabled, queer, poor). That theology, which developed within and is perpetuated by white Western Christianity, is the theological and moral foundation that drives white supremacy and racial capitalism. That theology runs in the veins of all our denominations, regardless of where we fall on the political spectrum.

So, if white supremacy is the structure of oppression, what does it look like, and how does it work?

THE FRUITS OF LABOR *(Figure 1)*

Imagine the structure of oppression as a pyramid. At the top are, to quote Martinez again, those of "wealth, power, and privilege." This top portion of the pyramid is comprised of a small percentage of the population, almost entirely white, cis/straight, and Christian, yet they hold a disproportionate amount of power. In the broad center of the pyramid are the middle, professional classes, and at the bottom, the working class and poor. As Iris Young points out, there is also a "marginalized" class, those people whose labor cannot or will not be recognized by this structure and who are then punished for being dependent on the state and charitable organizations and individuals for food, shelter, and other basic necessities. These include houseless, disabled, young, elder, and other people who are "expelled from useful participation in social life."[4]

There are two basic mechanisms of the structure of oppression:

First, through the exploitation of labor and extraction of resources including land theft, the fruits of labor are transferred from the working and middle classes, up to the wealthy owning class. This transfer of the fruits of labor is shown as an arrow driving to the top of the pyramid. While we may be aware of the exploitation of the working class, we may not think about how middle-class labor is being used to transfer the fruits of labor to the owning class—fruits which the middle class will often not see even though the structure offers benefits to the middle classes such as financial stability and health insurance, professional status, and some autonomy over their working conditions. These "benefits" function as a way to assure the middle class (especially the white middle class) that the structure is working for them. However, as we have seen during the COVID-19 pandemic, the student loan crisis, and skyrocketing housing and energy costs, those "benefits" are increasingly precarious, as they have always been for the poor and working classes, easily withdrawn when the wealthy and powerful so

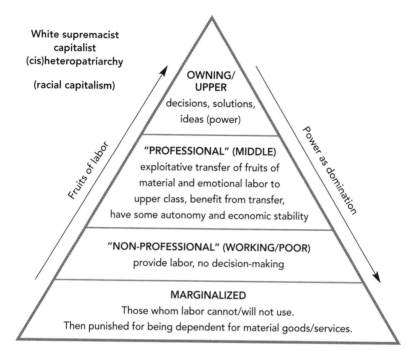

Figure 1: **THE FRUITS OF LABOR**

desire. The fruits of labor are both the profit and financial wealth made on the goods produced, whether those goods are a car, a tomato harvest, or armored tanks for police; and also fruits of emotional labor and domestic, menial, and service labor.[5] The fruit of emotional and service labor is important and often overlooked. Who is doing the emotional and physical labor so that the white wealthy class does not have to? Who is doing the cleaning, the landscaping, the schedule-keeping? Who is soothing the crying children, remembering the coworkers' birthdays, sewing the Halloween costumes? "Both indigenous people and the newly arrived slaves," says Rev. Dr. Willie Jennings, "were forced into the service of the white body. They cared for its needs and attended to its moods, its forms of desire, its ways of love."[6]

Second, dominating power is enforced down the pyramid—see the arrow driving down—by the wealthy class, both in order to control access to the fruits of labor and to control conditions under which people labor. For example, the wealthy and middle classes define what work is, what is "worthy" work, who works for whom and under what conditions, whose labor is valued/unvalued, who is considered a threat, and who is considered other. Labor is valued or devalued through laws, institutional rules and policies, funding or defunding of social services, and through narrative—the stories we both believe and tell about what kind of work is valuable.

This dominating power can appear benign, taking forms such as access to specialized knowledge in master's degree programs or the middle-class having health insurance and being able to set their own schedule. However, this power is also reinforced by violence—against race, against class, against gender, against gender expression, among other forms. We might immediately think of police violence, but we should also think of how schools arrest Black girls for violating dress codes or force Indigenous boys to cut off their braids; how hospitals neglect Black women's pain, sometimes to the point of death; how churches claim to welcome women and queers but always seem to pay them less when they become pastors; how city councils slash budgets for community services to invest in development, then stand idly by when poor folks are evicted from their apartments.

We sometimes call this basic structure racial capitalism.[7] White supremacy, race, and capitalism developed at the same time historically and are impossible to untangle. If white supremacy is the moral logic explaining why whites get to control labor and wealth, racism is what is used to define who is and is not allowed the fruits of labor. Race, as a category used to define people, was developed in the United States specifically to divide the poor and working class beginning in the seventeenth century. In particular, it emerged in response to European indentured servants and enslaved Africans building relationships, including intermarrying, as well as building power to improve working conditions. Wealthy landowners offered the benefits of a new category called "white" to the indentured servants, such as freedom, access to guns, and perhaps most importantly, the power to police and punish Black enslaved people for violating the conditions of their enslavement. This new category of "white" also established different standards of behavior for whites and non-whites. For example, an action considered criminal for an enslaved or Indigenous person, such as walking freely about town, was not considered criminal for whites. A poor white man might be fined or jailed for stealing; an enslaved man might be murdered. These different standards of behavior and punishment are roots of the violence in our structure and policymaking today.[8]

As we begin to explore this structure of oppression and the relationships of power within it, we should begin to see how white supremacy is not only about race, but also about gender, sexuality, gender identity/expression, class, ability/disability, and about who gets to define and control not only the value of goods and services, but also the value of a human life.

THE 3 PILLARS *(Figure 2)*

This pyramid didn't just come out of nowhere or simply evolve as some sort of natural next phase of human progress. When Betita Martinez says that white supremacy is "historically based,"[9] she means that people made *and make* choices in history that created and perpetuate this structure of oppression.

Martinez, Andrea Ritchie, and Andrea Smith all describe three "pillars,"[10] or essential conditions rooted in historical human choices, that are foundational to upholding the oppressive structure of white supremacy. These pillars illustrate the violent mechanisms and logics of this structure—the "how" of shifting fruits of exploitation/extraction

ORGANIZING FOUNDATIONS

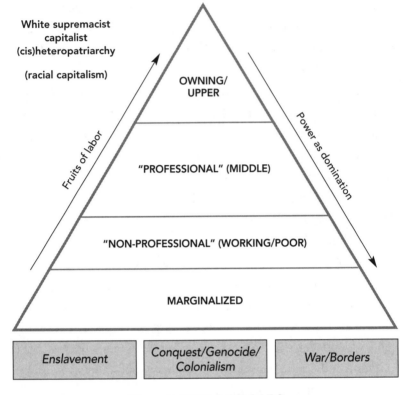

Figure 2: **THE 3 PILLARS**

to the wealthy, as well as the "why," the meaning that white supremacy makes out of these processes. Shown as three columns holding up our pyramid, they are both historically rooted and also continue to function to uphold white supremacy.

1. Conquest, Genocide, Colonialism

This pillar is the mechanism by which land and its resources are claimed in order to be extracted for wealth. It requires both genocide (killing, cultural erasure, displacement) and the perpetual disappearing[11] of Indigenous peoples to justify land theft. The logic of "permanent 'present absence'" Smith describes includes the erasure of

Indigenous history and place names, media blackouts against indigenous resistance, and cultural appropriation of indigenous practices.
"It is ok to take land from indigenous peoples," Smith asserts,
"because indigenous peoples have disappeared."[12] Another expression
of this logic is Manifest Destiny: the theology that the "US is destined
by God to take over other peoples and lands" and "the right of white
people to dominate everything around them."[13]

2. Enslavement

This pillar constitutes the view of Black people as always inherently
enslavable or property in order to assure access to free or cheap labor.
The mechanism of chattel enslavement morphed into the prison
industrial complex through the "Black Codes" during Reconstruc-
tion, Jim Crow laws, the War on Drugs, and the repression of Black
resistance through programs like COINTELPRO.[14] Its purpose,
though, remained the same throughout: to ensure access to that labor.
The meaning white supremacy gives to Blackness is that Black bodies
are inherently criminal, and thus deserving of control, surveillance,
and punishment. The logic of the criminalization of Blackness makes
sure the mechanism of enslavement—the access to free/cheap
labor—keeps functioning.

3. War, Borders, Imperialism

This pillar assumes that white supremacy, sometimes called "our freedoms," "democracy," "our way of life," "our jobs," and now during the
pandemic "our health," is constantly under threat and thus marks certain groups as inferior, as the "other," and as a threat. In the history
of the United States, these groups have included immigrants and
migrant workers, Latinx and Chicanx people, Asians and Pacific
Islanders, and those perceived as Arab or Muslim. All of these groups
are under suspicion of being "foreign" and a threat, regardless of their

documentation status in the United States. The logic of "constant threat" assures that companies who profit from war and border enforcement, including through arms and surveillance equipment sales, reap ongoing profits.

Each of these pillars functions to define and police whiteness: *who is considered white*, which is to say the one who can settle on land, the one who is not enslaveable or cannot be made into property, the one who is not a threat, and *who is not considered white*. The borderland of whiteness shifts according to white supremacy's need for labor, resources, and threats to achieve profits for the wealthy owning class. For example, Irish and Italians were not initially considered white when they arrived to the United States, but have now been assimilated into whiteness.[15]

Each of these pillars relies on binaries. White supremacy loves a binary, and these binaries are not neutral; they exist to enforce white wealth and power. Again, whiteness is happy to move the either/or boundary around *if* that shift serves white wealth and power. These binaries include:

- white – black
- settler – indigenous
- citizen – foreigner
- innocent – criminal
- man – woman
- straight – queer
- owner – exploitable
- abled – disabled
- well – mentally ill
- civilized – savage
- christian – godless
- normal – deviant
- cisgender – trans

You can probably think of more. *Just sit with those binaries for a minute.* Notice what you feel. Notice how they set up an ideal human on one side, and the lesser human on the other. Imagine what kind of story they are trying to tell, and about whom. What story they are telling about YOU. Again, these binaries aren't arbitrary or neutral. They create—invent!—a protected class—for example, male—and a class that violence is enacted upon—female. One purpose of the binary is to give reason to the violence.

Finally, each of these pillars also has a corresponding force of state violence to enforce it: police, military, border patrol and Immigration and Customs Enforcement (ICE), etc. They also control, surveil, and punish perceived violations of the binaries above. We need to be clear that these enforcement bodies, including the courts and the prison industrial complex, do not exist to keep us—whoever *us* is—safe, or to provide justice or accountability for harm. Rather, these enforcement bodies were created and continue to exist to uphold white supremacy and the meaning of whiteness (see chapter 12 on community safety).[16]

THE WISDOM OF BLACK WOMEN *(Figure 3)*

"If black women were free, it would mean that everyone else would have to be free since our freedom would necessitate the destruction of all the systems of oppression."

The Combahee River Collective[17]

Black feminists/womanists have always been clear that they live in "interlocking" oppressions[18] of race, gender, class, sexuality, ability, etc. Their radical politics are drawn directly from their particular lived experience that these oppressions are happening simultaneously and cannot be disentangled from each other. They insist that to be free of oppression means to be free of capitalism, racism, patriarchy, etc. all together. Represented by intersecting lines in figure 3, these interlocking

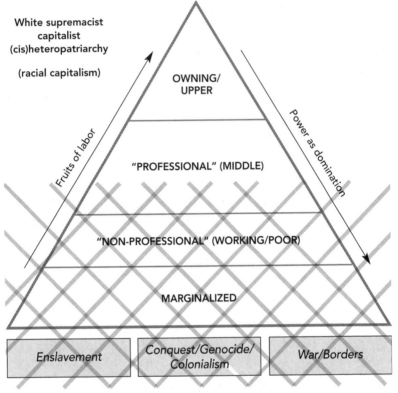

Figure 3: **THE WISDOM OF BLACK WOMEN**

systems mean we cannot address class without addressing racism, cannot address race without addressing sexism, and on.

Their wisdom points to the need to center the experiences of those most impacted by the structure of oppression in our liberation work, and the need to dismantle this structure and build something new, in which everyone is free and has all they need to thrive, rather than try to reform our way into a nicer version of white supremacy and racial capitalism. This is, in fact, the orientation of this book—to align ourselves with the wisdom, vision, and calls to action from Combahee's writers and leaders today: to practice disability justice, to build community care through mutual aid and trauma response, to abolish police, to protect our beloveds through sanctuary and community defense, to infuse our organizing with culture, to give land back, to have a clear analysis of power, to take action that builds transformative power, to assure our children and elders are involved and respected, and to invest in an economy in which everyone thrives.

A FEW MORE THINGS

In addition to the above, there are other logics that uphold this oppressive structure of white supremacy. Again, these run throughout our institutions, including our churches, and are why we keep perpetuating white supremacy in our institutions in spite of our best intentions. The structure of white supremacy relies on these logics, these stories we tell in order to keep it running, in order to keep the fruits of labor flowing into the hands of the white, wealthy, and powerful at the top. Here are a some of those logics; if we had a white board, we'd start adding them all around our pyramid:

- The characteristics of white supremacy culture,[19] such as perfectionism, urgency, order, worship of the written word, and the right to comfort, cause harm by promoting white supremacy thinking: highly individualistic, no room for risk-taking, an emphasis on production, valuing only certain kinds of knowledge, and defending hierarchical power.

- Work, productivity, and consumption are the only measures of worth within this structure, a cruel mathematics of extraction of our labor and the fruits of our labor. How much can you work? How much can you produce and consume? These capitalist evaluations care nothing for our tender, fleshy bodies and spirits that have limits, which need beauty and rest and care.

- Time is linear, marching ever onward towards human progress. There is no room for cycles of life and death, or for any emotion, or grief, or joy.

Take a breath here. Feel your body. In the blank space below, write down the names of people, of lands, of creatures you know who have been impacted in some way by this structure of oppression. How have the mechanisms and logics, the how and why, resulted in violence against them? Against you? Take a moment to speak their names and hold them all, including yourself, in love and compassion, and let your love for them drive your commitment to action.

WHAT DOES ALL OF THIS MEAN FOR OUR ORGANIZING

The ease of capital, the way it flows depends on a state that knows how not to love anyone. It teaches itself how to not love anyone by specifically hating and repeatedly sacrificing Black people. That is the story of capitalism. The lie we live each day even though we know the truth. Capitalism the long story of unlearning love. It can only work if we too forget to love each other. And we will not.

Alexis Pauline Gumbs[20]

One of the times I learned about the importance of focusing our action on dismantling the structure of white supremacy, rather than trying to "reform" violent institutions to be less violent, was when I collaborated with other grassroots leaders in Denver, Colorado to offer mutual aid to immigrants being detained in the private GEO detention facility in Aurora. As we were planning our work, one of the immigrant leaders used the framework of abolition to describe what we were doing.

Not everyone understood what he meant; I admit I didn't at first. He was gracious enough to explain. Yes, we were there because we were deeply concerned about how people being detained were being treated. But if our ultimate goal was not actually abolishing immigrant detention (and really, ICE as well), then all we were doing was trying to create nicer conditions for inhumane treatment. There is no "nicer" form of detention, because detention itself is inhumane; it's a form of state violence that upholds white supremacy.

So, our work focused on several forms of mutual aid: liberating people from detention by paying their bonds; visiting people whose families were in other states or who did not feel it was safe to visit; advocating for detained people who were being denied medical care; attending immigration court hearings so people would not be alone; and supporting families of those detained to assure they had food and shelter. In addition, as we talked with and listened to detained people and their families and friends, we learned more about the conditions inside the facility, the kind of mistreatment detained people experienced, the ways police and ICE colluded to fill detention quotas,[21] and other information that fueled our efforts to shut down the facility.

In other words, we built into our aid work ways to gather information that could inform our abolition work—we kept our vision and action on the ultimate goal of ending detention. The work is ongoing to shut down that facility, but some of that information we gathered was crucial to a statewide campaign that ended sheriffs' ability to work with ICE to send people to detention, and to repealing SB90, a state law that allowed police to question people's immigration status, which had also led to people being detained.

There is no "nicer" form of detention. There is no "nicer" form of white supremacy. The Covid-19 pandemic has surely taught all of us that white supremacy, that *this structure of oppression, does not love us, that it is happy to literally let us die rather than risk a loss of profits.*

Imagine a pandemic response where as many people as possible were assured the ability to stay home or have safe shelter, with food, medicine, and PPE provided at no cost; where health care was provided at no cost, including ample access to free testing; work and school simply pausing so that beloveds could rest and tend to one another in a time of immense fear and trauma; essential workers in health and food services actually provided with the safety equipment necessary to do their jobs; where no one had to risk losing a job if they became sick.

We had the resources to do this, to invest in the safety and well-being of all our people, to invest in alternative systems for collective care. For a brief moment it seemed like we might choose this...but racial capitalism does not love us. Investing in actual human well-being is a threat to the oppressive structure of white supremacy. Investing in the well-being of humans, the land, the creatures, is a threat to racial capitalism's bottom line and to white wealth and power. Thus, the fights over mask and vaccine mandates, over churches being allowed to ignore lockdown restrictions, over online or in-person schooling, while people continue to die, lose jobs, and be evicted, and unused vaccine goes wasted. Thus, free testing and vaccine sites being closed down because "we ran out of covid money" but millions keep being poured into policing and multinational corporations keep scoring higher and higher profits.

So, when we are organizing, let's keep this clear: *This structure of oppression does not love us.* And we don't have to love it back. Our goal must be collective liberation from an oppressive structure, and building up a whole new world of justice, compassion, and accountability, where all can live in safety and without fear, and where everyone has all they need to thrive.

BIBLE BLUEPRINT: Isaiah 58

This prophetic vision describes a whole re-built, re-structured society in which everyone has all they need to thrive. Written in the aftermath of the Bablyonian Empire destroying Jerusalem, Isaiah 58 is clear that simply rebuilding the same old system that oppressed workers and relied on violence while honoring an empty piety is not what God desires for us. Assuring that everyone has food, shelter, clothing, care, and community—that's what we are meant to build together, and in building that world, we repair (make reparation for) all that has been broken. *—Anne Dunlap*

Notes

1. The US support of the Salvadoran government's repression of the people's liberation movement is well documented. This support included weapons, training in torture techniques, CIA collaboration with Salvadoran military and support for military death squads and massacres of entire villages, financial aid, and support for assassinations such as that of Archbishop Romero in 1980 and six Jesuit priests, their housekeeper, and her daughter in 1989. For some examples of this involvement, I highly recommend Mark Danner's research into the El Mozote massacre in *The Massacre at El Mozote* (New York: Vintage, 1994), and School of the Americas Watch's resources at www.soaw.org.

2. In addition to decades of learning from grassroots Black, Indigenous, immigrant, QTPOC, and poor and working-class activists, organizers, and feminist, womanist, and liberation theologians in the US, Mexico, and Central America, I'm drawing on the work of these scholars/activists as well.

- Anne Braden, "A Letter to White Southern Women," 1972, https://newsreel .org/guides/Anne-Braden-A-Letter-to-White-Southern-Women.pdf.
- Combahee River Collective, "The Combahee River Collective Statement," in *How We Get Free: Black Feminism and the Combahee River Collective*, ed. Keeanga-Yamahtta Taylor, 15–27 (Chicago: Haymarket Books, 2017).
- Rosemarie Freeney Harding, with Rachel Elizabeth Harding, *Remnants: A Memoir of Spirit, Activism, and Mothering* (Durham: Duke University Press, 2015).
- Willie James Jennings, *The Christian Imagination: Theology and the Origins of Race* (New Haven: Yale University Press, 2010).
- Betita Martinez, "What is White Supremacy," https://collectiveliberation .org/wp-content/uploads/2013/01/What_Is_White_Supremacy_Martinez.pdf.
- Tema Okun's work on White Supremacy Culture, https://www.white supremacyculture.info/.
- Andrea Ritchie, *Invisible No More: Police Violence Against Black Women and Women of Color* (Boston: Beacon Press, 2017).
- Andrea Smith, "Heteropatriarchy and the Three Pillars of White Supremacy," in *Color of Violence: The Incite! Anthology*, ed. INCITE! Women of Color Against Violence, (Boston: South End Press, 2006), 66–73.
- Iris Marion Young, "The Five Faces of Oppression," in *Oppression, Privilege, and Resistance: Theoretical Perspectives on Racism, Sexism, and Heterosexism*, ed. Lisa Maree Heldke and Peg O'Conor, Peg (New York: McGraw-Hill, 2004), 37–63.

3. Martinez, "What is White Supremacy," 1.

4. Young, "The Five Faces of Oppression," 41.

5. Ibid., 40.

6. Rev. Dr. Willie Jennings, "The Geography of Whiteness," interview by Matthew Vega, *The Christian Century*, November 3, 2021, 24–27.

7. See the work of Ruthie Wilson Gilmore and Robin D.G. Kelly. See also Chanelle Gallant, "Screw Capitalism: For Love to Actually Win, We Need a Revolution," *Xtra Magazine*, July 19, 2021, https://xtramagazine.com/power/ capitalism-gay-marriage-205211.

8. For more on this history, see Robert P. Baird, "The Invention of Whiteness: The Long History of a Dangerous Idea," *The Guardian*, April 20, 2021, https:// www.theguardian.com/news/2021/apr/20/the-invention-of-whiteness-long-history -dangerous-idea; Quinn Norton, "How White People Got Made," October 17, 2014, https://medium.com/message/how-white-people-got-made-6eeb076ade42; Noel Ignatiev, *How the Irish Became White* (London: Routledge, 1995); Ritchie,

Invisible No More, 25–37. Bacon's Rebellion was a key turning point in the development of whiteness; see for example Robin D.G. Kelley's contributions in *Race: The Power of an Illusion*, "Episode Two: The Story We Tell," https://www .racepowerofanillusion.org/episodes/two; Michelle Alexander, *The New Jim Crow: Mass Incarceration in the Age of Colorblindness*, rev. ed. (New York: The New Press, 2013), 24; and "Inventing Black and White," *Facing History and Ourselves*, https://www.facinghistory.org/holocaust-and-human-behavior/chapter-2 /inventing-black-and-white.

9. Martinez, "What is White Supremacy," 1.

10. See Smith, "Heteropatriarchy and the Three Pillars of White Supremacy," 67–71, for "pillars." For the other trios of essential conditions, see Martinez, "What is White Supremacy," 1–3, for "three giant facts" and Ritchie, *Invisible No More*, 19–40, for "enduring legacies." While using slightly different language to address different organizing contexts, they are describing the same mechanisms and logics—the same how and why.

11. Smith, "Heteropatriarchy and the Three Pillars of White Supremacy," 68.

12. Ibid.

13. Martinez, "What is White Supremacy," 19–20.

14. See Ritchie, *Invisible No More*, 43–59, for one tracing of this mechanism's development.

15. See for example Baird, "The Invention of Whiteness."

16. See Ritchie, *Invisible No More*. See also Alec Karakatsanis, "The Punishment Bureaucracy: How to Think About 'Criminal Justice Reform,'" *Yale Law Journal Forum* 128 (March 28, 2019): 848–935.

17. From "The Combahee River Collective Statement," in Taylor, *How We Get Free*, 22–23.

18. Taylor, *How We Get Free*, 15; see also the work of bell hooks.

19. Tema Okun, "White Supremacy Culture: Coming Home to Who We Really Are," https://www.whitesupremacyculture.info/.

20. Alexis Pauline Gumbs, "It Takes What It Takes," blog post, April 22, 2021, https://www.alexispauline.com/now/2021/4/22/it-takes-what-it-takes.

21. See Detention Watch Network's amazing work here: "Detention Quotas," Detention Watch Network, https://www.detentionwatchnetwork.org/issues /detention-quotas.

2

· · ·

ORGANIZING CONGREGATIONS FOR IMPACT

· · ·

Marilyn Pagán-Banks

Without Community There is No Liberation
— Audre Lorde[1]

I recently ran across some minutes from a 2013 planning session for a faith-based organizing training, where I asked the question: *"How do we as pastors become movers of people vs. just pastoring in the confines of a building?"*

Little did I know that almost a decade later, I would be writing this chapter on community organizing for congregations while living and working in the midst of a pandemic and worshiping virtually for almost two years. The universe is teaching us—ready or not—how to be movers of people outside of our worship/gathering spaces if we are to truly BE the church.

CHECKING IN

I'm a queer womanist minister, healer, writer, and life-long co-learner committed to the liberation of oppressed and colonized peoples. I currently serve as executive director of A Just Harvest, which is a grassroots organization working to promote a just system to end poverty. I am also a pastor at San Lucas UCC and an adjunct professor at both McCormick Theological Seminary and Garrett Evangelical Theological Seminary. These aren't accolades but rather a testament to my experiences of the collective strength that defines the intersecting communities and congregations I have the opportunity to serve. Helping to pass the Pre-Trial Fairness Act as a part of the Coalition to End Money Bond was one way our congregation organized for impact. The purpose of this chapter is to encourage you not to be afraid to embrace organizing by moving beyond worship spaces. By the end of this chapter, you will understand how Jesus modeled organizing the collective power of voices and you will learn tools to organize your congregation for impact. First, let's talk about ways to pastor outside of spaces of worship and how to become a mover of people.

THINK OUT LOUD IN COMMUNITY

I'm an out-loud thinker and this shows up within and outside of worship spaces. Writing about organizing during a global pandemic is challenging. Writing about organizing during civil and racial unrest is challenging. Writing about organizing while struggling with depression and anxiety is challenging. Writing about organizing while people are dying due to gun violence, police violence, economic and environmental violence, homophobia, transphobia, xenophobia, capitalism, militarism, white supremacy...

...This is what happens when you ask someone who thinks out loud to write...endless thoughts and seemingly insurmountable challenges. This leads me to one of the reasons that community is so life-giving for me. In community I can think out loud.

BE IN COMMUNITY

Anyone who knows me would describe me as a community person. Community, as my chosen *primo* Patrick Reyes writes, "calls me to life."[2]

In community, I can lament and rejoice. In community, I get to think and imagine and reflect out loud. I learn in community. I find joy in community. I find hope in community. I find power in community. I find healing in community. In community I discovered my voice, and when I am most grounded in community, I become the clearest about my purpose. My community recognized my call to ministry and continues to affirm, shape, and challenge this call each day.

Learning about community organizing was the start of me fully embracing my call to ministry. I began to learn how to apply organizing methodology to my faith-based community, what I now know as faith-based community organizing. Faith-based community organizing was an organizing model championed by Gamaliel, founded in 1986, which used community organizing tools to train community and faith leaders to build political power. I learned how to show up in community.

I continue to work to decolonize the model that was passed on to me by pulling out the mostly white-male patronizing and savior behavior in which the methodology was rooted, and grounding the model in the creative and transformative power of love. Having always believed myself a *guerrera* (Spanish for warrior, and tattooed on my arm in the form of a machete!), I am doing the work of moving from warrior hero to warrior healer.[3]

ORGANIZE TO DISMANTLE

During my last year in seminary, the organizer of a faith-based institution reached out to clergy and other faith leaders and invited us to join a network being created to move those present to go beyond service and begin to organize to dismantle oppressive and racist systems in Chicago.

I had always been drawn to the work of social justice, but learning about the power of our collective voices as people of faith and the transformative power of the church as organized people really touched a place in me. I began to have a new and expanded understanding of the role of the church and learned the importance of building and engaging in deep relationships based on who we say we are and what truly matters to and for the community. My faith-based community and congregations organize to create spaces that also call community to life.

Faith-based organizing provided a methodology that would later become a *practice* where, as part of a collective, I could hold, make space for, put into action, and sustain the fire I had in my belly for God's people and all of God's creation.

> *It is our duty to fight for our freedom.*
> *It is our duty to win.*
> *We must love each other and support each other.*
> *We have nothing to lose but our chains.*
>
> —Assata Shakur[4]

COLLECTIVELY RECLAIM SPACE

Community organizing is *a daily practice* — a way of life that centers transformative relationships and fosters collective consciousness/ awareness, collective imagination, collective healing, collective power, collective action, and collective joy in the pursuit of collective liberation and love expressed in the world as the beloved community. My current working definition of collective: *an intentional sharing, gathering, and cultivating of gifts, resources, lessons learned, and vision for the world.*

Community organizing can seem scary to regular church folx. Some hear the words "community organizing" and immediately tense up or become anxious. For many, the words carry negative connotations, such as "outside agitator" or "too political." Others understand community organizing as something you leave to the "more radical."

Community organizing makes space for us to collectively reclaim, and when necessary, recontextualize language, words, and meaning: such as community, radical, power, political, resources, self-interest, money, tension, agitation, and anger.

I invite you to consider that Jesus embodied many of the characteristics of a community organizer that we sometimes fear

Jesus was an outside agitator.

He walked into towns not his own and often got into "good trouble," as the late Representative John Lewis would say. When Jesus saw an injustice, he would boldly and unapologetically call it out. He didn't limit his understanding of community simply to where he lived or to the people he came from. Jesus expanded the definition of community, and thereby our accountability to and for one another.

Jesus was political.

He took his faith into the public square and invited others to join in the building of the beloved community by loving one's neighbor as oneself. The Gospels are filled with story after story of Jesus taking risks, breaking barriers, crossing borders, and liberating his faith and all people from the oppressive stronghold of the Roman Empire.

One of my clergy colleagues in Puerto Rico said it in a way I have always found helpful. I was part of a UCC delegation that had come at the request of the local church to push for the removal of a US naval base that was poisoning the people and the water of Vieques, Puerto Rico with illegal explosives and that hosted a live munitions practice that killed a civilian. During the orientation, our host and colleague said that our choice to risk arrest through civil disobedience was in fact our choosing to be in obedience to the Gospel of Jesus Christ (see chapter 4 on direct action for congregations).

Before you worry that this somehow leaves you out—I offered this example but that does not mean that engaging in organizing necessitates risking arrest. There are myriad roles in the movement and room for everyone to participate in various capacities.

Jesus was radical.

According to Black-American political activist, philosopher, academic, and author, Angela Davis, "radical simply means 'grasping things at the root.'"[5] In other words, we have to understand the root causes of our conditions in order to be able to transform them. Jesus dedicated his life to naming and transforming conditions under which his people suffered. He lived and ministered with a radical faith lens, a radical anti-empire, anti-oppression, and anti-xenophobia lens. Jesus knew we needed to be the change and to *organize in order to transform the world by transforming our relationship with one another and our relationship with God.*

When I am challenged by congregations on why I organize and am asked what justice work has to do with Jesus (yes, I have been asked this—facepalm!), I remind folx that Jesus did not disrupt the social order by feeding the hungry—he was living out the tenets of his Jewish faith. This did not get him into trouble. Jesus caused conflict and tension when he started redefining neighbor, flipping tables, calling out the hypocrisy of certain religious leaders, and refusing to bow to the Roman empire—still living out his own faith. This got him crucified.

Jesus was an organizer.

Sometimes we fall into the trap of believing that engaging in advocacy and *advocating on behalf of others* is sufficient. While signing petitions, pushing "share" buttons, or sending that email letter to our elected officials does make a difference, these strategies alone are not sufficient in building the power of the community. Often, advocacy is done on an individual basis—safely from a distance—far from the horror and pain many others don't have the same privilege of distancing themselves from.

Unlike advocacy, organizing is hands-on—up close and personal. Faith-based organizing intentionally builds power *in* community, builds leadership, and shifts decision-making and power to the people. It builds and deepens relationships, community, and collective imagination.

Community organizing demands proximity. As Christians we should already know something about the importance of being there in the flesh, right? God modeled this for us in Jesus: Emmanuel, God with us. *Proximity matters!*

We, the church, are to be God's love and power made flesh in the world. We must reorient ourselves and do as Rev. Dr. Melva Sampson often charges during her weekly *Pink Robe Chronicles*[6]: "stop simply worshiping Jesus and start to actually follow Jesus."

Jesus spent a lot of time out on the block listening, seeing, noticing, taking in, asking questions, and making connections. And while Jesus did correct and provide instruction, he centered the community in everything that he did. Any correction or instruction was related to how to be in community—deeper community, intentional community, authentic community, a beloved and just community.

Jesus was able to reflect his concern and his care for community by his presence. Community organizing requires presence. The same way that the Word became flesh so that we might begin to be reconciled to God and to one another, so we too have to show up as Rev. Anne Dunlap says, with our *full fleshy selves.*[7]

The fight for justice is always too big for one person alone and we cannot win if we do not come together and organize. Jesus knew this. Jesus modeled this. He knew his gifts, operated in them, AND surrounded himself with folx with different experiences and different skills; then he began to organize and train them so they could do the work.

"Why do we fast, but you do not see?
Why humble ourselves, but you do not notice?"
Look, you serve your own interest on your fast day,
and oppress all your workers.
Look, you fast only to quarrel and to fight
and to strike with a wicked fist.
Such fasting as you do today
will not make your voice heard on high.

Isaiah 58: 3–4

ORGANIZING IS DISCIPLING

God's decree is clear here in Isaiah—what happens outside of worship and ritual *matters*. Discipleship needs to be reclaimed as what we do out in the community and not simply how we *do* church and grow our congregations.

If our actions in the public square, in our homes and communities, or as citizens of the world do nothing to usher in justice and care for the day-to-day needs of God's people, then we are not living into who we say we are and what we say we know about God.

Now, sometimes we get intimidated, and "thoughts and prayers" is as far as we ever get.

And this is not me trying to be extra churchy. This is me declaring that people are dying while too many of us are *playing church* or are only interested in creating new ways to *save the institution* we know as church. This is me calling BS and proclaiming TIME'S UP!

Providing meals is meaningful. We joyfully feed folx at San Lucas UCC in Chicago on a weekly basis. A Just Harvest feeds the community 365 days a year! Isaiah calls us to feed the hungry. Jesus directed the disciples to feed the people. But our ministry should not be limited to the privilege and safety behind the food serving counter.

Discipleship requires that our ministry include demanding that people not be hungry, by joining workers asking for a living wage on the picket line or getting on a bus to the state capital demanding a moral budget that protects the most vulnerable. If we do not, what do you think God would have the prophet say to us?

And notice I said "us." Because when we organize, it is all about the collective. It doesn't mean everyone has to be on the frontline, but it does require that we each do our part in creating powerful and strategic direct action. Romans 12:4 captures this point: Each member of the body has a unique role and purpose and is vital and necessary.

I once heard something at a clergy training that resonated with me, and although I can't recall who said it, I often use it when leading my own training: "We call it *community organizing* because it is the *community*, regular folx like you and me."

No special titles are needed. No degrees are necessary. No documentation is required. While in many spaces organizing has been "professionalized," it need not be for you to organize in your community.

Jesus knew that it would take everyone joining the movement—bringing what they had and a willingness to commit to develop the skills that perhaps they didn't have or hadn't honed yet. He trained his followers as leaders and then sent them out to do and build on the work he was doing—that's organizing!

I want to suggest that to move as followers of the One who came so that we "may have life and have it more abundantly" (John 10:10), we need to have a heart for the wellbeing of our community. This heart compels us to act so that our communities do more than survive and bounce-back—but thrive in love and life—and breathe free!

I absolutely love how the full essence of community organizing is captured within Assata Shakur's quote earlier: the power of relationship, mutual accountability, courageous love, thoughtful risk, and blessed freedom. This is life, more abundantly.

PRACTICING COMMUNITY ORGANIZING

Not too dissimilar from discipling church members, community organizing at its best uses an *asset-based approach*.[8] This approach starts by identifying and affirming the gifts, talents, experience, and resources of every individual. Through a generative process, leaders are trained and equipped to build transformative relationships, lead the work, engage in the public arena, and invite others to join in creating the world God desires for us.

So how does a *church* engage in community organizing? What I share here are overviews of community organizing skills. Many organizations offer trainings in these skills. Check out our organization list for possibilities!

The best way for a congregation to begin would be to start by organizing the congregation itself. For example, you might want to organize the fellowship committee to switch to fair trade coffee, or the congregation to hang a Black Lives Matter banner, or to engage in some piece of work this book calls you to. The same methodology used for community organizing is the same methodology that can be used *within the congregation*, because the more we can practice organizing ourselves, organizing our resources, and strategizing, the more effective we will be in being a part of the beloved community.

This includes building and deepening relationships through one-on-ones, building collective power, mutual accountability, action, evaluation, and reflection. We engage these practices, careful to keep in mind, as Dr. Gail Parker advised, that "It is more than just about the instruction, it is about the relationship."[9]

ONE-ON-ONES (1–1S)

Relationships are central to organizing. Relationships are central to life. We were not created in isolation nor are we to live in silos and in isolation. As we are reminded by the South African principle of *ubuntu—I am because we are.*[10]

Jesus did not work in isolation. Jesus knew the importance of relationships, of knowing the stories of the people, of connecting people to their own story—listening to and *reminding them of their story.* He made connections to their stories and to their experience and to the broader situation. He would ask questions and cause folx to pause, to reflect, and to question.

One way to build relationships is through one-on-one conversations. These conversations allow members to get to know one another beyond the surface, discover new leaders, and also learn what issues are breaking their hearts wide open for the community/world and/or directly impacting their own wellbeing and humanity. Organizing groups often offer one-on-one trainings, but they aren't magic. Here are some tips:

- One-on-ones center on listening and curiosity. Ask about experiences rather than opinions, and stories rather than ideas. Allow silence. Listen twice as much as you speak—and when you do speak, stick with questions, experiences, and stories. These conversations are about learning, not about converting someone to your point of view.

- A one-on-one can be a general ongoing practice in your congregational organizing and also a way to gather information about a specific project you are initiating; for example, you might do a time-limited one-on-one listening campaign to learn how people are thinking/feeling about the church organizing to stop police sweeps of unhoused folx.

- Build a team of leaders who are regularly conducting one-on-ones with the clear intention to hear and learn from members of the congregation. Practice some one-on-ones with your team!

- If you're doing a time-limited listening campaign, let the congregation know that the one-on-one team will be reaching out to set up conversations and explain why. Determine with the team if there are specific questions you'd like everyone to touch on. Then do outreach to set up conversations.

- Make some notes afterwards to share learnings with the team and protect people's confidentiality as needed. Make sure you have permission to share any identifying details.

HOLDING A COLLECTIVE VISION

Reflecting on what is shared and uncovered, the team begins to engage members in a process of strategically identifying the collective interests of the congregation. Interests in this context are best defined as *values or what matters*, and they are specific and clear. For example, it is in our collective interest to fight for climate change so we have a livable sustainable planet; or to fight to invest in mental health services rather than more jails because so many of us are impacted by mental health struggles. A congregation that is *clear about what constitutes its collective interest* is best equipped to powerfully carry out the work of the church in the public square. Organizing the congregation around its collective interest helps to build relationships founded on the trust and solidarity necessary in allowing them to act with a unified vision and strategy.

BUILDING COLLECTIVE POWER

Too often the church is unclear about power and our call to be powerful. We hear the word *power* and we cringe as visions of oppressive dictators come to mind. Or we come across folx we deem as powerful and behave powerlessly (often confused with *being humble*).

Beloveds, power is simply *the ability to act* in order to have our interests carried out in the world. The ability to do something when our communities are harmed. God has given all of us power (2 Timothy 1:7).

In organizing, power is built in two ways: organized money and organized people. The wealthy are able to influence policy because of money in politics. But we know from the recent wins in Georgia[11] that when people are organized around their collective interests and come out in numbers—WE WIN![12]

Reminding the community that those in powerholding positions work for and are accountable to us is one way to reclaim our power. Reminding those in these positions that they can be removed if they are not doing what is best for those they represent is how we claim our power and put it to work for the building of the kin-dom. These powerholders include politicians, church officials blocking the way for justice, businesses engaging in unfair labor practices, and more. This is about using our collective power so that our communities live and thrive.

Conducting a power analysis of all those with decision-making power, knowing who is pulling their strings or has their ear, and who is funding them, is how we show up equipped to leverage our collective power (see chapter 3 on power analysis). We can also do what organizers call "political education": intentional learning about how oppression and injustice are at work and impacting us.

Creating spaces where everyone is welcome is another way to build collective power. Tap into the interests and gifts of the community as they decide how they are able to show up. Sharing roles and dividing up tasks helps everyone to feel invested and able to contribute meaningfully.

MUTUAL ACCOUNTABILITY

Organizing work isn't easy. Being the church isn't easy. Organizing to dismantle white supremacy while simultaneously creating God's kin-dom here on earth is not easy.

Because organizing is all about *transformational* relationships: we commit to investing in each other's wellbeing. This requires walking with one another and a willingness to speak truth in love to one another. Sometimes that requires agitation.

When we agitate a person or group, we highlight the difference between who they say they want to be and how they are thinking or behaving. We do this from a place of deep relationship and mutual accountability.

Agitation is an act of love. We agitate people whom we care about so that they will get clarity and act on their values and become more powerful. Agitation is an act of courage it takes courage to tell a person or congregation the truth when you suspect that they may not want to hear it.

Agitation is effective but only in situations of deep or longstanding relationships and when you have received consent to hold the person and/or congregation accountable. Here is a congregational example:

A Just Harvest, where I serve as executive director, organized a congregation in the North Shore at their request; they wanted to help the village finally implement an affordable housing ordinance it had passed a decade ago. When some of the church members tried to challenge the work, the pastor reminded them of their mission to the poor and disenfranchised. The congregation had given him consent to hold them accountable. As had he with them.

He did not shame them, he lovingly reminded them. The congregation came together, organized the village, and the ordinance was finally implemented. Folx who traveled from across the Chicago metropolitan area, commuting for hours to get to work, could now afford to live in the village many of them served and labored in daily. Many were women, Black, brown, and immigrant/refugee folx. *¡Sí Se Puede!*

ACTION

If power is the ability to act, then action is the way to show your power. In Vieques, the direct action was civil disobedience, and in the North Shore of Chicago, it was a large group showing up unexpectedly to a village board meeting demanding to be heard because all other attempts at getting the ordinance implemented had gone ignored. Direct action is a key element of transformational change.

See chapter 4 about organizing direct actions. Here's a quick tip though: If you want folx to engage in direct action, or any action for that matter, you have to organize them. Bulletin or Facebook announcements are not enough! Remember, organizing is about relationship building, which requires direct and repeated contact. One-on-one conversations are one of the most effective forms of engagement.

EVALUATION AND REFLECTION

In my organizing training, I learned that "anything worth doing is worth evaluating." Taking the time to collectively debrief and evaluate meetings, actions, and events continues to affirm the investment and leadership of each person involved. Creating brave space so folx know they are heard also helps to minimize messy communication leading to misinformation and misunderstandings and "parking lot conversations" after the meeting ends.

The format I learned has four parts:

1. *Feeling Word*: What has this experience caused you to feel or how has it left you feeling? One feeling word that comes from your gut or is reaction based. Not a head word like informed or interested.

2. *Performance*: This includes everyone who had a role first evaluating themselves and then inviting feedback on what went well and where there was room for improvement. This can also

include logistics, space, etc.—anything that had anything to do with the flow of the thing you are evaluating and folx want to name happen here.

3. *Tension*: Did you experience any tension? When? Why? Tension is a good thing. It helps us to stretch and causes us to act. I use the example of a rubber band. When it is sitting on the desk, it is useless. When it is picked up and stretched, it can help hold things together, be wrapped around important things, or keep your child's braids in place.

4. *Political learning*: What was heard during the evaluation that can be applied and help us to show up all the more powerful and faithful in the public space for the good of God's kin-dom here and now?

PERSONAL AND COLLECTIVE REFLECTION

Each person involved in community organizing needs to spend time reflecting. This is separate from prayer and meditation. This is the intentional practice of asking ourselves on a regular and scheduled basis: Are my actions consistent with who I say I am? What is affecting my behavior?

Engaging in regular and scheduled strategic reflection as a collective asking the same questions is also important in congregational organizing for ensuring accountability and movement.

MOVE YOUR CONGREGATION FOR IMPACT

Jesus reminds us of the two great commandments: Love God and love your neighbor as yourself. Let's use these commandments as our lens and litmus test in our organizing. Because unfortunately, sometimes even those of us on the path towards justice can get caught up and become bitter. We don't always do enough ongoing work to continue to decolonize our own practices, our own behavior, or our own thinking and we can remain oppressive, judgmental, patronizing, and disempowering in our work.

And so, we must check our privilege as church folx. We need to check our assumptions. We need to be in touch with our own trauma. And we always need to be willing to be transformed by our connections and to engage in our own healing practices. We are not called to save communities; we are called to walk alongside, accompany one another, and truly understand that the liberation of my sibling is tied to my very liberation.

Ashé, Selah, and Amen

BIBLE BLUEPRINT: Luke 10: 1–9

Jesus sends not twelve, but seventy people he has taught and trained out to do the work of healing, teaching, and sharing food together. This means Jesus built collective power by organizing the people so that the work of healing, teaching, and feeding would have an even bigger impact. This is what it means to be disciples: to think and move like organizers! And to realize we cannot do this work alone.

—*Anne Dunlap*

Notes

1. Audre Lorde, "The Master's Tools Will Never Dismantle the Master's House," in *Sister Outsider: Essays and Speeches* (New York: The Crossing Press Feminist Series, 1984), 112.

2. Patrick B. Reyes, *Nobody Cries When We Die: God, Community, and Surviving to Adulthood* (St. Louis, MO: Chalice Press, 2016).

3. See the description in: Stephen Lewis, Matthew Wesley Williams, Dori Grinenko Baker, and Parker J. Palmer, *Another Way: Living and Leading Change on Purpose* (St. Louis, MO: Chalice Press, 2020).

4. Assata Shakur, Angela Yvonne Davis, Lennox S. Hinds, *Assata: An Autobiography* (Chicago: Lawrence Hill Press, 2001).

5. I heard this definition shared while listening to a Girl Trek Black History Bootcamp Walking Meditation this past summer. For more information go to www.girltrek.org.

6. Pink Robe Chronicles, https://www.drmelvasampson.com/pink-robe-chronicles.

7. Rev. Anne says this a lot and said it on one of our planning calls with the contributors to this book.

8. For more information on asset-based approach, check out the ABCD Institute at DePaul University, Chicago https://resources.depaul.edu/abcd-institute/about/Pages/Values.aspx.

9. I am paraphrasing a quote from a lecture with Dr. Parker on Sunday, September 12, 2021. She was discussing her book, *Restorative Yoga for Ethnic and Race-Based Stress and Trauma* (London: Singing Dragon, 2020).

10. See Sakiemi Idoniboye-Obu and Ayo Whetho, "Ubuntu: 'You Are Because I Am' or 'I Am Because You Are'?", *Alternation* 20, no. 1 (2013): 229–47.

11. Organizing efforts led by Black women, voters shifted the state from red to blue.

12. See for example this piece on the importance of deep conversations to identify collective interest in flipping Georgia: Marcy Rein, "Can We Crack the Right's White Bloc? These Organizers Say Yes," *Convergence*, January 12, 2021, https://www.organizingupgrade.com/can-we-crack-the-rights-white-bloc-these-organizers-say-yes/.

3

. . .

POWER ANALYSIS FOR
POWERFUL CONGREGATIONS

. . .

Ayanna Johnson Watkins and
Lucy Waechter Webb

We experience power in the broken system of domination
(either as dominator or the oppressed [or both]),
and then feel like we want nothing to do with it.
There, we have to reimagine what collective power looks like.

—Vanessa Moses, Causa Justa/Just Cause[1]

What is the first image that comes to mind when you hear the word power?

Was it a person? A memory? An organization? A feeling?

What are the words you would use to describe that image?

Notice if those words are more negative or more positive.

Before we can talk about power analysis, we first must address power. We were taught by organizers from the Gamaliel Network that power is simply: the ability to act.[2] Yet, our guess is that most of your responses to the questions above may have leaned toward the negative.

People not in traditional positions of power tend to be allergic to the notion of having power. Since the dominant systems in the United States often only have room for a few to be powerful, many have experienced power primarily in painful and oppressive ways. Thus, many tend to shun power—even hate it. As the quotation above describes, we are bombarded with power that is toxic: power that terrorizes, oppresses, excludes, and abuses. It rests with a few and is lorded over the many.

Organizing, however, depends on the reality of *another* kind of power: collective power. It is the power of the people, shared equitably among the people, and used for the good of the people. It is built on solidarity—standing together united in purpose. With it, we can borrow courage from one another and share the risk. Collective power desegregated public transportation in Montgomery, Alabama. Collective power built among farmworkers in California increased workers' rights and working conditions. Collective power across the nation in solidarity with Indigenous leadership defeated the Keystone Pipeline. Collective power liberates and transforms.

Jesus of Nazareth was a brilliant community organizer who built collective power. He began at the margins, tending to those most impacted by the toxic power of the occupying Roman empire. He transgressed boundaries that were racial, geographical, religious, and class-based, and formed a coalition across difference—even including some who were complicit in upholding the status quo. After building relationships *with the people*, hearing their stories, tending to their pain, and preaching a vision of liberation, he turned to face the center of toxic imperial power to challenge the roots of oppression *alongside the people*.

Jesus did not have to move this way. Considered by Christians to be both God and human, he could have stayed separated from—even elevated above—the people. Instead, the One called Christ:

Who, being in very nature God,
did not consider equality with God something to be used to his
own advantage;
rather, he made himself nothing
by taking the very nature of a servant,
being made in human likeness.

—Philippians 2:6–7 (NIV)

Jesus chose to stand with the people most affected by the world's evil and manifest a divine power they themselves could possess — power that would outlast his brief time on earth. As Christians, we are taught this was both gift and example. As the verse immediately before this passage instructs, we are called to "have the same mindset."

Yet, he could not have stood with humanity and exercised such power without considering how power was operating in his environment — from the Roman government officials to their local governors and tax collectors, from elite Jewish leaders willing to betray fellow Jews to act as an extension of Roman power, to Sanhedrin officials working from the inside to make way for Jesus's justice movement to thrive. Jesus paid attention to who decision makers were, where ordinary Jews and Gentiles could be organized for collective power, and where traditionally powerful people could be swayed from social domination to communal equity. In organizing circles, we call this *power analysis.*

WHAT IS A POWER ANALYSIS?

Ayanna: One of my first experiences in organizing was working with a group of primarily African-American clergy affiliated with a local community organization in Chicago. One community concern we addressed was gun violence among young people. As clergy, we felt the burden of this issue. We officiated the funerals and consoled the families of loved ones lost to gun violence. We worked closely with young people who lived surrounded by violence—mentoring, tutoring, even feeding and clothing them—to try and steer them away from joining gangs and using guns to resolve conflicts. At countless vigils we mourned our children who we lost to death and incarceration because of gun violence, adding their names to an ever-growing banner of names outside one of our churches.

As we gathered to strategize, we initially asked the questions we often hear in public discussions about gun violence and youth: "Why are black youth killing each other?" "How can we stop young people from joining gangs?" "Where are the parents?" Then the questions got a little deeper: "Why are these young men on the corner instead of working or going to school?" "What makes gang affiliation attractive/necessary?" "Why must parents work two and three jobs to keep a roof over their children's heads?" Eventually, we asked: "How are these young people—too young to be registered gun owners—even getting guns?" In other words: "Who is selling guns to *children?*"

That question catalyzed the group. We understood there were multiple contributors to gun violence in our communities. But the question about the *source of the guns* helped us to name that somewhere the mechanisms ostensibly meant to protect us had failed, and that to address that failure meant identifying *who has the power to fix it, and who benefits from things remaining just as they are*. Though the pain for our community was immense, we had to take seriously the hard realization that it was also someone's—or multiple someones'—gain.

What we were doing was the very beginnings of a power analysis.

A power analysis is the act of looking for *who* and *what* stands between us and the change we seek. It involves determining who wants the change we seek, who benefits from keeping things as they are, who could be swayed, and the relative ability (power) of each to affect the outcome. Power analysis is a key aspect of the strategic work of organizing; it helps us make concrete plans for specific change. An effective power analysis will identify particular people as well as policies, practices, attitudes, institutions, and systems that can manifest, accelerate, influence, or impede the change we want to see.

Power analysis involves asking questions about our communities: Who has the stated "official" power? And who do those people listen to? Who controls access to the changes we want? What's important to those who hold that power? What power do we have to affect those decisions and make our community a place where we can thrive?

WHY DO POWER ANALYSIS?

Ayanna: I do not have a green thumb. I have a gorgeously caramel brown thumb, which has proven largely incapable of getting anything to grow. Still, from time to time, I find myself outside in the yard, puttering about with a new packet of zucchini seeds or a handful of collard green sprouts my mother-in-law gave me to try planting. Despite my sad track record for growing anything, I have gotten better at pulling weeds. As many of you already know, the key to pulling weeds is to get them out with their roots attached. If you leave all or part of the root in the ground, the weed will simply grow back.

Pulling weeds the other day, I noticed that some weeds had super short roots and were easy to pull out. Others, though, had long, wiry roots that spread out far beyond what I could see above the surface; I was grabbing a six-inch weed and pulling its roots out three and four feet at a time and still more was left in the ground. Instead of growing straight down, these roots grew largely horizontally, snaking back and forth across the entire length of the garden bed—choking out healthy plants before they even had a chance.

Trying to make systemic social change without doing a power analysis is like trying to remove weeds while leaving their roots in the ground. You can tame the problem for a short while, but it will grow back.

TO GET AT THE ROOTS

Ayanna: One tool for thinking about a power analysis is the Weed Diagram, which uses the image of a weed in the ground to represent an issue or problem we want solved. This is a tool created by another organizer I admire, Mahal Burr.[3] The diagram has four parts:

- The Look (flower/bloom): the presenting issue, or what *appears* to be the problem. "How does it manifest?"

- The Stem: the Trick: the apparent causes of the issue, or who is typically blamed for the issue

- The Roots: the Cause: the true cause(s) of the issue. "What is really causing this to grow/stay in our communities?"

- The Nutrients: Deeper Cause: "What is feeding or sustaining the causes?"

Burr's Weed Diagram helps us resist easy and surface-level explanations for the issues we face. It reminds us that the look and stem

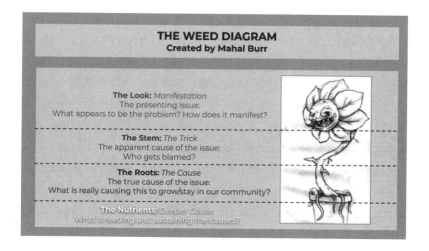

THE WEED DIAGRAM
Created by Mahal Burr

The Look: *Manifestation*
The presenting issue:
What appears to be the problem? How does it manifest?

The Stem: *The Trick*
The apparent cause of the issue:
Who gets blamed?

The Roots: *The Cause*
The true cause of the issue:
What is really causing this to grow/stay in our community?

The Nutrients: *Deeper Cause*
What is feeding and sustaining the causes?

are just the face of the problem—Black youth violence (look) seems to come from what is often referred to as Black-on-Black crime or wayward youth with absent parents (stem). But the root and nutrients of the problem involve decades of government-sanctioned destruction (urban renewal, imminent domain) and disinvestment (redlining) in Black neighborhoods, legal protections for gun shops and other businesses that benefit from illicit gun sales, elected officials whose campaigns are financed by these same businesses and industries, the racist assumption that Black people are naturally more violent and thus nothing can be done, and so on.

Just as with any living plant, the real lifeblood of that organism is below the surface. To do power analysis, we have to be willing to dig in the dirt—searching out past and present people, practices, and policies—to identify the roots and what feeds them. Sometimes the roots aren't deep, and it just takes dealing with a few people or practices to unearth and solve the problem. But other times, and maybe most of the time, the roots are long and tangled—involving systems and relationships that stretch far beyond the original issue and will take a lot to untangle.

TO UNDERSTAND HOW POWER MOVES

Lucy: Most of the time I have found it dizzying to sort out the layers of who has power to do what in the public arena. Once you finally figure out what power the prosecutor holds or untangle the complicated relationship between the way the city and county mayors interact, there is yet another layer of discovering the hidden influencers who can impact those who have the ability to act.

One of the best ways to get a feel for these layers is to examine the power of a system you may already know more intimately: your faith community. Many of us know the list of "official" people who make decisions within a congregation: the board/trustees/elders, the staff or regional leaders. Many of us *also* know exactly who we need to talk to, convince, sway, or outvote to make a controversial decision — and often the former list of names is not the same as the latter. Maybe you want to move the American flag out of the sanctuary, or maybe you want to leave your doors unlocked to the community during the week. Even if those with stated power might be able to *technically* make the decision, there are likely others with hidden power who can influence whether or not those changes are actually made.

The last church I served as pastor made the painful decision to sell their building. The formal sale took place before my arrival, and early in my ministry there we were still moving out of the old sanctuary. As we did, there was one story I heard over and over again. It was a story about power.

The congregation had wrestled for years about what to do with their property as well as their failing budget and declining spirit. Over a decade, they explored a variety of options, and as they neared a crisis point with their budget, the elders knew they needed to act. The governing laws of the Presbyterian Church USA leave the power of decision-making regarding property of the church to the Session (the church board). The members of that board, however, were wise enough to know that this decision was too important to be made around a table with twelve people. They voted to forward the decision to the congregation and called for a congregational meeting to hold a vote.

They gathered one Sunday after worship in the fellowship hall with much discussion, angst, and uncertainty. The body was not yet unified in a decision. And then Ladye Margaret stood up. Ladye, as she was affectionately called, was the matriarch of the church who had previously been married to one of the most beloved pastors in the church's history and had separate family ties to the founders of the congregation. She was deeply respected for the way she served as a leader, *and* if there was a decision made that didn't sit well with her then you'd better sit up and pay attention!

That day, as Ladye rose to her feet, the room was uncertain what she would say. Since several people in the older generations were some of the most hesitant about the sale, many assumed she would speak against it. Instead, she gave a rousing speech about how selling the property was a hard and painful decision, and yet it was the right one. She grounded her support for the sale in faith and scripture, in the history of the congregation itself, and said we must do this together. And then she sat down.

The congregation voted that day, and all but two people voted to move forward with the sale.

This story illustrates the important realities of *stated power* and *hidden power*. If the Session had made the decision to sell the building without the congregational vote, they would have been well within their rights but might have lost half the congregation. They recognized there was hidden power, power among the members, who could have taken their bodies and their money elsewhere. I don't think any of them fully realized the weight of the hidden power Ladye Margaret held until all was said and done.

While such hidden power in the hands of one person can be used at times to block forward movement, it can also be used to bring the community along. One of the people who contributed to my own training as a community organizer, Greg Galluzzo, put it this way: "[A community is] an ecosystem that has hidden parts. A snake that is hidden might bite if you touch it or step on it the wrong way. A certain [hidden] plant you may find might be medicine."[4] A good power analysis helps us to understand and navigate our ecosystems for the sake of building collective power and using it in transformative ways that manifest our shared values.

HOW DO WE DO A POWER ANALYSIS?

One of the most common tools used for power analysis is power mapping. This visual tool helps us to name who may affect our issue and place them on a map according to the amount of power they wield and how aligned or opposed they are to the change we seek.

Start by asking some of the following questions, placing specific names or groups in one of the four quadrants of the power map. Think of each aspect as a spectrum; for example, you may not know whether a powerful individual agrees with your position or not, so you may place them toward the top and in the center. Part of your analysis would then need to include research about how they may align with your stated issue.

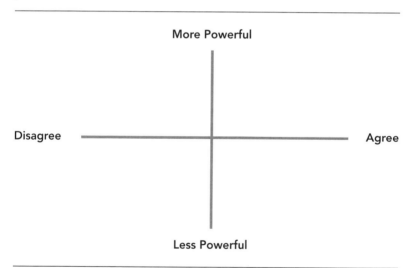

More Powerful

Disagree — Agree

Less Powerful

Questions to ask for power analysis:

What is the problem/issue we have identified?

Who has stated power to make changes in this arena?

Who holds that person accountable?

Who advises, influences, funds that person?

Who else is that person connected to personally?

What institutions/groups are they a part of?

Who is blamed for this issue? Who benefits from it?

What material and cultural realities in the institution/society perpetuate this injustice?

Who is already organizing around this issue?

Who is directly impacted by the issue?

Who are the not-yet-organized who could potentially affect the outcome?

Asking the right questions can lead you both closer to your targets for action and to better questions. It also helps you to think creatively about how you might influence change.

Lucy: For example, while doing death penalty abolition work to restrict the use of capital punishment for those convicted of a capital crime who also had mental illness, I learned that a governor had a brother who had mental illness. Knowing that governor's personal connection to this aspect of our campaign was critical as we strategized about messaging and personal meetings with him.

When mapping power, it's also critical to name the systemic social codes (the "nutrients") that feed the issue. While no one campaign can end white supremacy in America, naming the power of white supremacy behind each individual issue keeps you focused on demands that will ultimately lead toward abolition of white supremacy. As Rachel Herzing, founder of Critical Resistance put it:

"Stop doing reformist reforms that will need to be undone later; instead, what are abolitionist steps that you can be taking?"[5]

A good power analysis does multiple things:

- Helps us get clear about what we need and want, who and what stands in the way, and who and where allies are or could be developed.

- Reminds us that there are human beings behind every decision.

- Looks for both stated and hidden power: people holding public positions and official roles and those who influence them and our issues.

- Explores how a decision-maker moves and is moved by the ecosystem; exploring multiple options to change their behavior is critical (for instance, personal pressure, public pressure, identifying shared interests).

- Identifies institutional/systemic barriers that stand between us and change; people hold power *and* systems of oppression operate from a place of power (for example, white supremacy and colonialism).

- Remains fluid—recognizing that ongoing analysis can cause strategy to evolve over time.

- Believes in the power and heart of God. Divine or spirit power can turn an unjust situation around, even when we are seemingly outnumbered and out-resourced.

THEOLOGY AND POWER ANALYSIS

Why should congregations do this work? Because we are in the ecosystem of power.

Power is neutral, but *our* power is not. Power is neutral when it is latent; once it is incarnational, embodied by people and (people in) institutions, it does one of two things: it upholds the status quo, or it actively works to change the status quo. Not engaging in an issue is still a choice to passively uphold the status quo. We must choose what our role is going to be.

While there is definitely a technical dimension to this work, it is also deeply theological. In the Christian tradition, there are many examples of God's people facing oppression and injustice. Yet, the constant refrain in our scriptural tradition is that righteousness, truth, and justice matter deeply to God. God has consistently empowered the marginalized and oppressed to prevail over the circumstances and enemies that threaten their wellbeing.

As Christians, we can lean into the life of Jesus for examples of how power analysis shows up in the gospel narrative. In Jesus's healing stories, he highlights how the "look" of paralysis, blindness, or incessant bleeding cannot be addressed by blaming the "stem" of personal failure or sin. Instead, these material conditions must be addressed at the root, which in this case was the oppressive Roman Empire. That oppression manifested as overpriced and ineffective healthcare, social bias against those living with disease, and the extraction of resources and money from the poor and working class.

The religious authorities, those with access to healing, had to navigate their own survival in the face of Roman repression. The chief priests were appointed by Rome, and some chose to align and assimilate with Rome, while other members of the Sanhedrin remained in critical opposition. All were assessing the landscape of power, and all were managing trauma because of Roman occupation (see chapter 8).

Jesus saw this power dynamic, read it accurately, and protested collusion with the empire by offering healing directly to those who needed it and reinstating them as valued members of society. In doing so, he challenged both the power of the Roman Empire and its collaborators to dictate who could be healed and whose life mattered. He even damaged property in the process (Mark 11:15–18)!

ANALYZING OUR OWN POWER

Recognizing our own power can sometimes be an obstacle for the faithful. Many of us were shaped by traditions that prized a selfless humility—a relinquishing of self-determination in the name of not becoming too proud. We were taught to think of power as bad, evil, dangerous. Power is what the prideful seek, not the faithful. Power is the currency of politics, not faith communities. And we are included among those who, as pastors and organizers, have struggled with our relationship to power when organizing for social justice.

* * *

Lucy: I have wrestled with my relationship to power. In my organizing training, I was encouraged to consider that I had power and how I might step into it more fully. I was pushed to identify what might be getting in the way of feeling that truth, and time and again, the phrase that came to mind was that I was, simply, *small potatoes*.

I had big ideas, I had strong opinions, I had deep relationships with those most impacted—shoot, I had even done my research about some of the issues, but I still felt . . . I'm just *small potatoes*. I thought my congregation was too small to be influential at city hall. I was a young-ish cis-female pastor trying to save a dying church that had just moved out of its historic building; no one even thinks we're legit. (Who thought Jesus was, anyway?) No one would care what we think or say. I just needed to shrink from public view and work hard behind the scenes to support those who were already fighting.[6]

This internal narrative allowed the status quo of how toxic power functions in our society to win. It allowed those who are in power to intimidate me, and it allowed the false notion that those with titles are always the best candidates to lead in a particular area. I minimized the voices of my own congregation, including my own, and remained isolated from building true collective power with those around me who were also doing the work.

It also meant that I was outsourcing my power to institutions and systems that are broken. Rather than coming alongside my community to think about what keeping each other safe looks like or ensuring everyone has enough to eat and a place to sleep, I was relying on institutions that are not actually caring for my neighbors to figure it out. I have huge gratitude for my comrade in this struggle, Nichola Torbett, for first helping me to see how I had given my own power away to the very systems I do not trust. As she says, "When we stop outsourcing our power for change to those systems, relationships become the alternative. And we were built for that."[7]

I had become allergic to the notion of power because all I had experienced was power in a system of domination and oppression. I have since tasted the beauty of collective power, and work daily to stand in my own power for the sake of participating in the struggle for collective liberation.

This is a call to action for congregations to stop outsourcing your power and instead get your hands in the dirt—using power analysis to root out what is killing our communities and strategize for lifegiving change. This is a call to ground that action in our faith with Jesus's own ministry as an example of a fierce and irresistible embodiment of power—a movement in pursuit of healing, wholeness, and liberation that unapologetically sought to overturn the status quo. People of faith must resist the temptation to align ourselves (individually or institutionally) with oppressive empire; it does not bear life! Instead, we are calling on our faith communities to acknowledge the power they already have and apply it as a force for collective liberation. Many spiritual traditions, including Christianity, affirm: our own spiritual wellness is bound up in the liberation of the whole. The good news is we can all get free together!

BIBLE BLUEPRINT: Philippians 2:5–7

Jesus was and is powerful. Not just spiritually powerful, Jesus served powerfully while on earth. Powerful in community. Powerful with and alongside the people. Powerful in actively resisting oppressive forces. Powerful in rejecting what does not resemble love. How we seek and wield power speaks to having the same mindset of Christ. "He became like one of us." May we become powerful like Jesus, together. —*Vahisha Hasan*

Notes

1. Vanessa Moses, panel speaker at Visionary Organizing Strategies Panel hosted by the Catalyst Project on June 1, 2019, https://www.facebook.com/watch/live/?v=298484314430352&ref=watch_permalink.

2. For more information about the Gamaliel Network, whose mission is to "empower ordinary people to effectively participate in the political, environmental, social, and economic decisions affecting their lives," see https://www.gamaliel.org/.

3. Mahal Burr. Used and adapted with full permission.

4. In-person trainings for MICAH (Memphis Interfaith Coalition for Action and Hope) with Greg Galluzzo, 2018, Memphis, TN.

5. Hear Rachel Herzing, Vanessa Moses, and Ash-Lee Woodard Henderson in a powerful panel discussion on Visionary Strategy hosted by The Catalyst Project Anne Braden Anti-Racism Training on June 1, 2019 here: https://fb.watch/2QR49r54J2/.

6. For white people engaged in the work of justice, particularly campaigns with antiracism at the core, this is not a bad strategy nor an instinct to be ignored. At the same time, it can function as an excuse for not taking risks and not stepping into our own power and leveraging our privilege. This is a delicate balance that must always be acknowledged and examined, with the support of accountability partners who are Black, Indigenous, and people of color.

7. Nichola Torbett, Showing Up for Racial Justice (SURJ) Faith Webinar October 14, 2020: "Community Safety for All: Launching the Congregational Action Toolkit." Webinar can be accessed as "Toolkit Launch Webinar" here under "More Resources:" https://surj.org/our-work/surj-faith/cs4a/.

4

. . .

IT'S TIME TO SET IT OFF
Direct Action for Congregations

. . .

ERICA WILLIAMS

*Christianity is being concerned about others, not building
a million-dollar church while people are starving right around the
corner. Christ was a revolutionary person, out there where it was
happening. That's what God is all about, and that's where
I get my strength.*

—Fannie Lou Hamer[1]

On November 6, 1996, the chart-topping movie *Set It Off* was released.
It started my journey to answer the question: "What would you do to
be free from the vicissitudes of life?" The movie stars Queen Latifah,
Jada Pickett Smith, Vivica Fox, and Kimberly Elise portraying four
Black women from a ghetto in Los Angeles. The women are low-wage
workers dealing with systemic racism, police brutality, homophobia,
and gender violence. They have been through hell and back and
know that nobody is coming to save them. Therefore, they take matters into their own hands.

The four women, whom I would describe as lionesses, decide to
rob a bank to secure money so they can live to see another day. They

study and survey their prey and know the right time to strike to set it off. Their plans allow them to gain some freedom, but ultimately the police stop them by killing all the women except one, who they spare because they feel guilty for having wrongfully killed her brother. This film showcases the plight, fight, and insight of poor and marginalized communities around the world. What we see in the movie are the same things we see happening in our world today, and it brilliantly displays for the world what it means to take direct action to make those who have perceived power realize that you will not be forgotten but free.

As a faith leader watching this film I wondered where the church was in the midst of the women's struggle. I noticed that the creator of the film did not mention religion one time. If I were to take a wild guess, I would assume it was because too often, the church is more concerned about heaven and not the hell people are living in here on Earth.

WHAT IS DIRECT ACTION?

In the urban dictionary the term "set it off" means to start a fight; to get into it.[2] This is the opposite of what most church people want to do. They mostly want to pray and wait for someone else to do work. Fannie Lou Hamer said it best: "You can pray until you faint, but unless you get up and try to do something, God is not going to put it in your lap."[3]

To set it off is to take direct action. When people's backs are against the wall, pushing back against oppression becomes inevitable. The term direct action means that we take collective action to change our circumstances.[4] The goal is to make people say yes to your demands when they really want to say no. This requires people to put their bodies on the line, which could lead to arrest as well as personal, institutional, and social backlash. Direct action is people coming together across lines of difference to force unjust rulers to do the moral thing, creating a strategic plan that brings results.

This work has been happening for centuries, including how the liberator Jesus Christ gave us a blueprint in his inaugural message in Luke 4:18–19, when he boldly declared that he came to disrupt the status quo:

> *The Spirit of the Lord is upon me,*
> *because he has anointed me*
> *to bring good news to the poor.*
> *He has sent me to proclaim release to the captives*
> *and recovery of sight to the blind,*
> *to set free those who are oppressed,*
> *to proclaim the year of the Lord's favor.*

Basically, Jesus told them: "I'm not here to be a chaplain of the empire but a prophet of God. I'm here to disrupt business as usual and to set it off!"

Jesus, a brown-skinned Palestinian Jew, a carpenter whose work was exploited. He grew up in Nazareth, a town which was mostly poor, and like all of Palestine, was ruled and militarized by the Roman Empire. A man whom society considered a nobody *set if off* by showing radical love and revolutionary compassion, and by speaking truth to power. He did not do it by himself. Rather, he organized a fusion coalition who even after his lynching continued to *set it off* by organizing and building power to confront, challenge, and change the systems of injustice.

This lineage of moral disrupters has continued to build throughout history. This includes people from various faith traditions. One of the leaders who emerged was Rev. Dr. Martin Luther King, Jr. He saw the needs and plight of the people and knew that he could not remain silent against the injustice. Dr. King stated, "Any religion that professes to be concerned with the souls of people and is not concerned with the slums that damn them, the economic conditions that strangle them, and the social conditions that cripple them, is a spiritually moribund [at the point of death] religion."[5]

Rev. Dr. Martin Luther King, Jr. eloquently answers the question of why people should engage in nonviolent direct action in his Letter from Birmingham Jail. "You may well ask: 'Why direct action? Why sit-ins, marches and so forth? Isn't negotiation a better path?' You are quite right in calling for negotiation. Indeed, this is the very purpose of direct action. Nonviolent direct action seeks to create such a crisis and foster such a tension that a community which has constantly refused to negotiate is forced to confront the issue. It seeks to dramatize the issues that can no longer be ignored. My citing the creation of tension as part of the work of the nonviolent-resister may sound rather shocking. But I must confess that I am not afraid of the word 'tension.'"[6]

Direct action is integral to the mission of the church and it is past time that the Body of Christ take deep introspection to assess if it is standing by or standing up against the injustice in the world. The question I have for the church is: which side are you on?

THE CRITICAL CALL FOR THE CHURCH TO SET IT OFF

The Bible contains numerous commands from God to the people to be the moral authority in the land and to ensure that those who are impacted by oppression are not ignored. Jeremiah 22:1–3 declares God's orders: "Go down to the house of the king of Judah, and speak there this word, and say: Hear the word of the LORD, O King of Judah sitting on the throne of David—you, and your servants, and your people who enter these gates. Thus says the LORD: Act with justice and righteousness, and deliver from the hand of the oppressor anyone who has been robbed. And do no wrong or violence to the alien, the orphan, and the widow, or shed innocent blood in this place."

God's children are dying all over the world at the hands of corrupt leadership in government and counterfeit clergy in the church. People around the world are crying out for freedom and we must do our part in making justice a reality and not just rhetoric. It is time for us to not only celebrate and commemorate what folks did years ago but also become relevant by helping to usher in this new earth that is being shaped.

When I became a minister of the gospel in 2010, I promised God and the Ancestors that I would put my hand to the freedom plow and not let it go. Seeking to maintain this stance has not come without challenges. Moving from the rhetoric of justice to the reality of justice costs. When you commit to being a follower of Jesus, one who is willing to flip tables or speak truth to power, it will cost you something. Jesus admonishes us in Luke 14:25–31 to count the cost before we go into the battle. This journey is long and hard and many days I want to quit. However, I am reminded of the great cloud of disruptors that have come before me and I take solace in knowing that I am not alone and help is available.

Direct action is directly connected to my ethos of radical love. Under the guidance of the Holy Spirit, I recently launched a ministry that will engage in direct action as a way to set the captives free. Set It Off Ministries is an international, interfaith, intergenerational ministry that empowers, educates, and emancipates poor and working-class communities around the world. This ministry organizes people from both faith as well as non-faith traditions in order to build power to fight systemic injustice. Our role is to help restore wholeness to those who have been abandoned by society. We are a movement following in the revolutionary footsteps of Jesus Christ.

We understand that we cannot do everything to change the world, but we will do our part. Our first direct action was on Pentecost Sunday, May 31, 2020, five days after George Floyd was lynched by the police in Minneapolis. At the time I was living in Raleigh, North Carolina, where many people protested in solidarity with folx in Minnesota as well as to bring awareness to all those who had been killed by the local police department. Set It Off Ministries had been working with local grassroots organizers in the city and was asked to support the protests. I put a call out to folx from various organizations in North Carolina to come together for prayer downtown at the capitol building, followed by standing as a shield of protection between the police and the protestors. The police were throwing tear gas and shooting rubber bullets at people as they marched to the governor's mansion to demand policy changes for racial equity.

This work continued for many months as the ministry provided food, housing, and donations for the organizers and the community. As a result of coming together, the people agitated the Governor of North Carolina to veto Senate Bill 168, which would have shielded police from accountability for murder, and to address the misconduct by the Raleigh Police Department during the uprisings. Finally, they helped ensure the removal of Confederate statues that were housed around the state capitol building.

EXAMPLES OF DIRECT ACTIONS

There are many ways to engage in direct action. Direct actions do not have to be public in the traditional ways, nor do they necessarily require people to be arrested. Below are a few examples of direct action that can take place in congregational settings or public squares[7]:

- Graffiti/Murals
- Marches
- Strikes
- Blockades
- Creative Disruption
- Social Media Storms

- Boycotts

- Sit-ins

- Rallies

- Civil Disobedience

- Pilgrimages/Lamentation

- Flash mobs

BASIC STEPS TO ENGAGE IN DIRECT ACTIONS

This chapter is not a substitute for getting trained in the tactics! See our organization list for groups that you can reach out to for training in direction action. These are the steps Set It Off Ministries took as we planned our actions in 2020.

1. As a congregation, decide what issue(s) you have the capacity to engage with. Do not try to do everything.

2. Connect with grassroots leaders in your community who are already working on the particular issue you identified. Then ask if you can talk with them about ways that your church can support their work. Please do not go into the conversation telling people what you will do. The point is to listen and get clarity on the ways you can use your platform to promote the cause. This is not about getting notoriety for the pastor or the church. This is to expose the plight of the people.

3. Get trained in direct action tactics. Again, check out the organization list in this book.

4. Decide with the community what type of direct action you would like to take.

5. Collectively, with grassroots leaders and impacted folx, create a list of demands for the action: What are we asking for?

Research the various policies that impact the particular demands. Make sure you have data/background information that supports the issue you are standing against. As Bishop William Barber II says, "Nothing is worse than being loud and wrong."[8]

6. Research who the "target" is for the action. Who is it that has the power to make the changes you are asking for? For example, it could be the mayor, city council, governor, business owner, church body, etc.

7. Create a disciplined plan for the action. Once the group decides on the action they are taking, then discuss the various roles needed to ensure things move smoothly. Possible roles include the following:

   a. *Legal Team:* This group has some basic knowledge of laws and includes someone(s) who can deal with police if they show up. This group can also observe and record police actions and violations of people's rights. Please work with local social justice-oriented lawyers to provide pro-bono work for the actions if needed. For more information on movement lawyers, please check out Forward Justice.

   b. *Lead Organizers:* Two to three individuals who will help to lead the group during the action. They are the designated group who makes decisions during the action.

   c. *Cultural Organizing:* Music, art, and culture are central to the work of building a campaign and are essential for moving people's hearts and minds (see chapter 10). They are some of the most powerful means we have to unite people across differences, help share the message of the campaign, and build a collective identity. Music, art, and culture can help build confidence and courage in challenging situations, and they help shape the atmosphere and set the stage for prophetic speaking.

d. *Marshals*: A group that varies in size depending on the size of the action. Marshals help to facilitate the direct action as planned: to act as an information source for planners, lead organizers, and demonstrators; to help demonstrators be safe and feel good about demonstrating; and to act as a buffer between police, hecklers, and bystanders. Please visit https://actupny.org/documents/Marshall.html for a sample guide for marshals.

e. *Medic Team*: A group with some medical training or at least health and safety training with some basic medic supplies or trained certified street medics (see, for instance, the Do No Harm Coalition).

f. *Jail Support Team*: A group who has their group's contact information and will work to get their friends out of jail and connect them with a lawyer. Some in this group will also be at the jail waiting for folks to be released and will have food and medical care for them. This group is "non-arrestable" if they are present at the action, which is to say that the leaders know this group cannot be arrested if at all possible. Sometimes some or all of this group are offsite, for example at home, and are in touch with designated leaders such as marshals as the action unfolds.

   a. "Non-arrestable" folx can also include those who have identified that they will not be arrested at this action.

g. *Vibes Watchers*: This group makes sure everybody is doing well and keeps up the energy in the group via chants or songs. Of course, everyone in your group should keep an eye on each other!

h. *Media Contacts*: The group prepared beforehand to speak to media (see below).

8. Prepare your media outreach strategy. Have you identified and prepared media spokespeople who are committed to the campaign and can effectively communicate about the campaign and the event? How will you create your own media? Examples might be writing letters to the editor, creating videos or memes, and social media engagement.

9. Conduct the action. The day after, debrief with the group. Devise a plan for next steps.

10. *Rest.* Please make sure the group does not burn out. Please prioritize the wellbeing of the participants (see chapter 8). Saint Oscar Romero said it best in his poem "A Future Not Our Own": "We are prophets of a destiny not our own."[9] Therefore, we must remember that we will not solve all of the problems we are facing.

IT'S YOUR TIME TO SET IT OFF

As June Jordan declared, "We are the ones we have been waiting for."[10] *No one is coming to save us, not even Jesus.* He already did the assignment he was sent to do. Now it is up to us to do our part and pass the baton to the next generation. We *must* come together and work together for the liberation of all oppressed peoples around the world. May we each know in our hearts that each of us have been called for a certain purpose and collectively we can make a difference. There is a song in the Black church that says, "I need you to survive." Will you rise and roar in your own way like those four lioness did in "Set It Off" to ensure that those who have been left out by society can find shelter in the storm?

Let us go to the Spirit to ask for divine guidance as we *set it off!*

Creator in your infinite mercy and grace give us the strength and courage to be doers and not just hearers of your word. Let us be swift to stand against the empire and the injustices we see. Let us not continue in our complacency of playing it safe while the breath that you gave to your people is being deflated each day by the systems of poverty, racism, militarism, ecological devastation, our nation's distorted moral narrative and Christian nationalism.

Help us, Great Liberator, to set our face towards injustice like *Jesus* set his towards Jerusalem (Luke 9:51).

Lead us as we go down like *Moses* to places of injustices and declare boldly, "Let our people go" (Exodus 5:1).

Grant us the spirit of *Esther* that said, "I will go to the king, though it is against the law, and if I perish, I perish" (Esther 4:16).

Let us persevere like *The Persistent Widow* who pressed on until she made the unjust judge grant her demands (Luke 18:1–8).

Make us steadfast like *Stephen*, who continued to confess your word even in the face of death (Acts 7).

Strengthen our backs like *Fannie Lou Hamer* who declared "Sometimes it seems like to tell the truth today is to run the risk of being killed. But if I fall, I'll fall five feet four inches forward in the fight for freedom. I'm not backing off."[11]

Solidify in us which side we will be on like *Rev. Dr. Martin Luther King Jr.*, who declared: "I choose to identify with the underprivileged. I choose to identify with the poor. I choose to give my life for the hungry. I choose to give my life for those who have been left out. This is the way I'm going. If it means suffering a little bit, I'm going that way. If it means dying for them, I'm going that way."[12]

Ignite in us a holy fire like *Harriet Tubman*, who encouraged those escaping enslavement: "If you hear the dogs, keep going. If you see the torches in the woods, keep going. If there's shouting after you, keep going. Don't ever stop. Keep going. If you want a taste of freedom, keep going."[13]

Mold in us the mindset of *Mother Jones*, who professed: "I am not afraid of the pen, or the scaffold, or the sword. I will tell the truth wherever I please."[14]

Organize us so that we can declare like *Ella Jospehine Baker*: "We who believe in freedom cannot rest until it comes."[15]

Help us Holy One, to keep our eyes on the prize until we see justice roll down like a mighty stream.

Amen, Ase', Blessed Be

BIBLE BLUEPRINT: Luke 9:51, Exodus 5:1, Esther 4:16, Luke 18:1–8, Acts 7

As you go through these Bible verses from the litany, reflect on how you might be called to direct action in your own community.

Notes

1. Dante Stewart, "Singin' Us to Glory: The Life and Legacy of Fannie Lou Hamer," October 6, 2017, https://thewitnessbcc.com/singin-us-glory-life-legacy-fannie-lou-hamer/.

2. "Set It Off," Urban Dictionary, https://www.urbandictionary.com/define.php?term=Set%20it%20off.

3. Keisha N. Blaine, "'God Is Not Going to Put It in Your Lap': What Made Fannie Lou Hamer's Message on Civil Rights So Radical—And So Enduring," Time, October 4, 2019, https://time.com/5692775/fannie-lou-hamer/.

4. "Theory: Direct Action," Beautiful Trouble, https://www.beautifultrouble.org/toolbox/#/tool/direct-action.

5. Martin Luther King, Jr., "Address at the Religious Leaders Conference on 11 May 1959," The Martin Luther King, Jr. Papers Project, http://okra.stanford.edu/transcription/document_images/Vol05Scans/11May1959_Addressatthe ReligiousLeadersConferenceon11May1959.pdf.

6. Martin Luther King, Jr., "Letter from Birmingham Jail," in *The Radical King*, ed. Cornell West (Boston: Beacon 2016), 127–46.

7. See more examples at "Tactics," Beautiful Trouble, https://beautifultrouble.org/toolbox/tactic.

8. William J. Barber II, "Here's Why I Got Arrested," *Sojourners*, April 18, 2016, https://sojo.net/articles/why-i-got-arrested-us-capitol.

9. "The Romero Prayer," The Archbishop Romero Trust, http://www.romerotrust.org.uk/romero-prayer.

10. June Jordan, "Poem for South African Women," http://www.junejordan.net/poem-for-south-african-women.html.

11. "Fannie Lou Hamer," Americans Who Tell the Truth, https://www.americanswhotellthetruth.org/portraits/fannie-lou-hamer.

12. "Quotes from Rev. Dr. King's Last Years: 'A Revolution of Values,'" Kairos Center, https://kairoscenter.org/quotes-from-rev-dr-kings-last-years/.

13. "Harriet Tubman Quotes," Black Alliance, https://blackalliance.org/harriet-tubman-quotes/.

14. In Linda Atkins, *Mother Jones: The Most Dangerous Woman in America* (New York: Crown Publishers, 1978).

15. Lea E. Williams, *We Who Believe in Freedom: The Life and Times of Ella Baker* (Raleigh: North Carolina Office of Archives and History, 2017).

SECTION II

. . .

Crucial Building Practices

5

. . .

COME AS YOU ARE
Possibilities for Dreaming Disability Justice in Congregational Contexts

. . .

JADE PERRY
EDITING BY RACHEL T. BLAKES

*Disabled people have always existed, whether the word
disability is used or not. To me, disability is not a monolith,
nor is it a clear-cut binary of disabled and nondisabled.
Disability is mutable and ever-evolving. Disability is both
apparent and non-apparent. Disability is pain, struggle,
brilliance, abundance, and joy.*

—Alice Wong[1]

There is no perfect way to "do" disability justice in congregational organizing. It is my hope that naming this straightaway gives you room to meet
me outside of the white supremacist cultural notion of "perfection."[2]

There is no one way to be disabled or chronically ill. There is no
one way to have a body. It is my hope that naming this straightaway
allows you to meet me beyond the binaries of sick versus well.[3] It is
an invitation into the fluidity of your own body.

There will be no tidy checklists of "things your congregation can do for disabled folx." Our shifting bodies necessitate shifting strategies. Disability justice organizing happens in non-linear time. We wait for each other. We make sure each other's bodyminds[4] are provided for. We act like we want each other in the room . . .

On the program . . .

In the pulpit . . .

Beyond the pulpit . . .

What we have is this moment. What we have is each other. What we must do is dismantle ableism in our personal lives and public initiatives. And in order to do that, we must be clear on the insidious nature of ableism, learn the context of disability movement-making, and come to embrace the power of community/collective care. It is my hope that this chapter helps us to either begin or continue that work.

But first, an honest review to ground our work together.

* * *

I was invited into this project as a Blackqueerdisabled femme organizer attempting to survive capitalism just as the COVID-19 pandemic began. To be clear, I am not a parishioner, clergy member, or regular attendee of any institutional church. So, this chapter found incubation space in group texts with other Blackqueer chronically ill women of faith over a great span of months. It was written in "crip-time"—an intercommunity term meant to convey a nonlinear time signature that makes space for bodies to be bodies. For feet to swell. For backs, arms, wrists to ache. For chronic fatigue demanding more rest, comfort, and care.

Time passed and the global COVID-19 pandemic stretched on (and on), and I watched folks struggle and debate on whether to wear masks on a national level. The disproportionate impact of COVID-19 on Black, Brown, and Indigenous communities was felt as family members, friends, and loved ones fell ill.[5] Disabled community members reeled from the impact of largescale gaslighting: national downplaying of the pandemic, new accommodations made for able-bodied people that were often denied to disabled folks pre-pandemic (for instance, working from home), and deeper isolation.

How does one write on any kind of sophisticated disability justice organizing while predominantly white neighborhoods across the city insist on maintaining outdoor brunch? When colleagues, collaborators, and community members have passed away and *are* passing away in droves? When folks are dealing with the privatization of care due to the medical industrial complex (hospitals, big pharma, wellness industries) and with the ways folks individualize care because of this?

Much has changed in this COVID-19 moment. Perhaps even our own bodyminds have changed, as has our orientation to time (as in the now commonplace question, "what day is it again?"). Perhaps, we have come deeper into the realization that *all of our bodies have access needs*—ideal conditions, norms, and provisions that keep us safe and cared for. Perhaps it has illuminated a sense of responsibility toward collective care and caretaking. But perhaps we are still ignoring the access needs of our collective body . . . of our own body. Prioritizing productivity in the midst of a global pandemic has meant eyes bloodshot after long hours of screen time. It has prompted us to apologize for things like going to the bathroom, eating, and drinking in the presence of others, as if these things weren't biological needs.

In 1980, Audre Lorde wrote ironically, "Whenever the need for some pretense of communication arises, those who profit from our oppression call upon us to share our knowledge with them. In other words, it is the responsibility of the oppressed to teach the oppressors their mistakes."[6] In 2020 (through a pandemic and management of my own chronic illnesses), I was crafting chapter outlines again and again, trying to find ways to amicably say, "Ableism is killing us and we need a revolution."

It turns out, however, that the best way to say something is to say it.

Community lawyer, prison abolitionist, and political organizer Talila L. Lewis defines ableism in conversation with Disabled Black folx (namely Dustin Gibson) as:

> A system that places value on people's bodies and minds based on societally constructed ideas of normalcy, intelligence, excellence and productivity. These constructed ideas are deeply rooted in anti-Blackness, eugenics, colonialism and capitalism. This form of systemic oppression leads to people and society determining who is valuable and worthy based on a person's appearance and/or their ability to satisfactorily [re]produce, excel and "behave." *You do not have to be disabled to experience ableism.*[7]

Simply put, capitalist production, forced legacies of labor rooted in the enslavement of African peoples, Western Christianity's notion that the body's needs, wants, and desires are "base"—all of this is death dealing. The pressure on our bodyminds to continue performing "business as usual" is ableism. It is also unsustainable. The refusal to wear a mask during a global pandemic is ableism. It's also death-dealing. Pastors' insistence for parishioners' bodies to meet in-person during a global pandemic is ableism. It comes at the detriment of each person, disabled, non-disabled, or somewhere between the spectrums. "You do not have to be disabled to experience ableism."

Now, after months and months of national health crises and failing medical systems, any contributions that we might make in terms of disability justice must be more than theoretical. Focusing on one-time accommodations for individual parishioners during in-person church services won't be enough in this moment. We cannot three-hour-webinar our way through this. This is also a good place to reflect on whose bodyminds these one-time accommodations privilege and whose bodyminds they exclude. It is an invitation to ask ourselves if the expectations placed on our bodyminds are ones rooted in deep respect or in grind culture.

Although it's been a while since I've been in the weekly fellowship of the saints, I've spent considerable years of my life there. I'm sure that in light of our times, the congregational church has changed. It now stands with the task of dreaming new norms, new ways forward, ways that center the health, access, and care of all of its parishioners.

*   *   *

To begin forward movement, we must first go back. This is the African diasporic value of Sankofa, symbolized by a bird looking backward, gathering a pearl in its beak. There is wisdom to be gained by looking at the flow of social movements from the past to the present. Doing so helps us to dream of our more just future. The following section will unpack a few key flash points on the road to disability justice, the medical model of disability, and the social model of disability. Then, we'll consider how disability justice might look in your local context.

In the 1960s, the disability rights movement came into fruition, inspired by the organizing strategies signature to the political movements of the time. Its primary concerns included legal rights for disabled persons, as well as the creation of advocacy organizations, direct service agencies, membership-based organizations, and cultural and academic spaces for disabled persons. However, this movement only focused on one identity[8] and so did not unpack the specific struggles of folks who were multiply marginalized. It wouldn't be until 1989 that legal scholar Kimberlé Crenshaw would introduce the notion of "intersectionality" into the field of law.[9] The term would help us to unpack our own social identities (race, gender, nationality, sexuality, ability, socioeconomic class, religion, etc.) and to understand the concept of multiple marginalization for years to come. In fact, this notion would become a core theme of disability justice work in later years.

There are a few ways that our dominating culture and institutions might view the concept of "disability." The *medical model of disability* proposes that a person's specific bodily symptoms or limitations are the primary cause of "disability." In this view, disability is fixed (you either are or aren't disabled) and illness or disability is seen as *an individual issue* needing *individual accommodations, treatments, and/or medical interventions.*[10] In the medical model, the goal often includes "cure," as defined by the medical practitioner.

The *social model of disability* proposes that we all hold a variety of body realities and/or limitations. Society can become systemically *enabling and/or disabling* depending on its concerns, priorities, and relationship to accessibility. In this framework, wellness and accessibility are dependent upon the collective instead of the individual. Therefore, each individual has a range of choices which may or may not include treatments, medical interventions, etc.[11]

Understanding these frameworks might also help us to make an assessment of the ableism present in our dominant norms. It also prompts us to think about how we view care, care work, and collective access, which are just a few principles of the disability justice movement.

In 2005, the disability justice movement was seeded by "disabled queers and activists of color"—namely Patty Berne, Mia Mingus, Stacey Milbern, Leroy Moore, Eli Clare, and Sebastian Margaret. The movement started with a framework, one that "understands that all bodies are unique and essential, that all bodies have strengths and needs that must be met. We know that we are powerful not despite the complexities of our bodies, but because of them. We understand that all bodies are caught in these bindings of ability, race, gender, sexuality, class, nation state and imperialism, and that we cannot separate them."[12]

In plain speak, we aren't doing the work of disability justice if we aren't centering these communities. The landscape of healthcare, environmental racism, and the political realities of the multiply marginalized have everything to do with disability. Our disability justice work, then, should not be separate from the comprehensive work of justice.

The Sins Invalid disability justice primer *Skin, Tooth, and Bone* offers a wealth of resources and historical knowledge on disability movement-making. For the purposes of this chapter, I will simply list the ten core principles of disability justice and trust the reader to do their own deeper research.

10 PRINCIPLES OF DISABILITY JUSTICE[13]

Intersectionality
Leadership of Those Most Impacted
Anti-Capitalist Politic
Commitment to Cross-Movement Organizing
Recognizing Wholeness
Sustainability
Commitment to Cross-Disability Solidarity
Interdependence
Collective Access
Collective Liberation

To be clear, the church is not doing disability justice work unless it has a working understanding of these principles. For example, a disability justice–centered response in this COVID-19 moment would not only engage the basic collective access needs of parishioners. It would also prompt clergy to consider how the COVID-19 virus disproportionately impacts Black and Brown communities.[14] An *intersectional* approach considers that, "prior to the pandemic, people of color had higher rates of health conditions, were more likely to be uninsured and face barriers to accessing health care, and were more likely to have lower incomes and face financial challenges. These underlying disparities put people of color at increased risk for exposure to the virus, experiencing serious illness if they are infected, and facing barriers to accessing testing and treatment."[15] Under the *leadership of those most impacted*, clergy and parishioners might organize a robust and *sustainable* mutual aid fund to cover medical costs. Further conversations would include ways to organize toward *collective access* to healthcare, regardless of income or insurance status.

Through disability justice we can seek to understand and uproot ableism, recognize our body's inherent worth outside of capitalist production, and foster collective access and liberation. It is this framework that we will keep in mind as we look at how specific congregations might organize.

Understanding the dominant models and norms in your church (institutionally and congregationally) is an important place to begin the work of organizing. You cannot organize from a standpoint of ignorance. You also cannot organize and simultaneously distance yourself from the concept that your own liberation is entangled with the liberation of disabled folks. So, it helps to take an honest look at the current prevailing norms in your organization and whose bodies, minds, and realities they center.

* * *

In the section that follows, your congregation will be prompted to sit with a number of questions. They will help you to gauge the disability justice ethic in your congregation. It is my hope that you will engage them with sincerity and courage. In order to do this, you might need to search for further information. You might like to hold conversation circles with others or incorporate this into a Zoom meeting or livestreamed program at your church. Grappling with these questions will help your congregation to better understand what your current practices are and who they center.

- How has your pastoral team responded to the collective access needs we hold in the COVID-19 moment?

- How has your denomination and/or congregation responded to these access needs on larger scales?

- What theologies, thoughts, or reflections have ministry leaders given on the topic of disability justice, if any? (If none have been offered, feel free to reflect on why that might be.)

- How do ministry leaders discuss Biblical characters that might be read as "disabled"? Are they active agents in their own stories? Do reflections reinforce binaries of "sick" versus "well"? Is healing (physically, spiritually, emotionally, and socially) conflated with cure?

- Whose responsibility is it to ensure that disabled members' access and accessibility needs are met? (If you don't know the answer, that is an answer.)

- What initiatives are in place to ensure that collective care and mutual aid are fostered?

- What are the public sentiments that have emerged from your denomination and/or congregation on accessibility and disability? How does the language point towards or away from disability justice?

- Given the makeup of your church's leadership, are you able to regularly hear decisions, needs, and theological views voiced by disabled folks?

- How does your church offer liturgy and sacraments? Map out the process. Reflect on whose bodies might be included and/or excluded.

- How are church services offered? Whose bodies does this create space for? What adjustments might be made (for instance, closed captioning, transcriptions, accessible websites and technology, etc.)?

- How are your organizing activities offered? Whose bodies do they create space for? What adjustments might be made (for instance, closed captioning, transcriptions, accessible websites and technology, actions that don't rely on marches, etc.)?

Pause to note how this process made you feel. Not in some distant future. Right now. What came up for you and in you? Where have you bought into ableist notions of worthiness, productivity, and/or excellence? When have you benefited from them? When have you been harmed by them? How have you perpetuated them?

*　*　*

My lived experience as a Blackqueerdisabled femme includes the blessing of a learning from a lineage of collective care workers in the Black charismatic church. I didn't always have the language of access intimacy—a concept coined by disability justice advocate Mia Mingus[16]—to describe moments in which all parties make loving efforts to build access, safety, and care. Access intimacy is not offered begrudgingly. It goes beyond accessibility checklists into making space that honors the flexibility of the access needs we hold. I'd like to offer a few anecdotes on what access intimacy looked like in a small church in the Mt. Airy neighborhood of Philadelphia called New Testament Assembly (NTA).

NTA was technically a nondenominational space, but it functioned as a Blackpentecostal church—a portmanteau coined by Dr. Ashon Crawley to describe the ways that Blackness and Pentecostalness function and move together as "transformational energies carried in the flesh."[17] Crawley posits that "to breathe . . . from within the

zone of Blackpentecostalism, is to offer a critical performative intervention into the western juridical apparatus of violent control, repression, and yes, premature death."[18] In this text, the aesthetics or the
performance of breath and breathing in the sermonic moments allow
us to critique the ways that racistcapitalistimperialism halts our breath
and our ability to thrive. *I would argue that it was this precise ethic
that allowed access intimacy to become woven into the fabric of the
space.* If a performance of breathing was a Blackpentecostal norm and
preaching style, then it found its expression in the ways that folks
cared for each other's physical bodies inside and outside of the
church's four walls.

Every Sunday, in my childhood to my teenage years, my family
packed up the van and drove forty-five minutes into the city to fellowship with about forty other members. And that was on a good day. The
building sat up on a steep, concrete incline where the parking lot (and
after-church lounge) was. It was a small building, perhaps a residence,
turned into a community funeral home, turned into a church. After
many years and an exterior coating of Pepto-Bismol pink paint, it
became known as the New Testament Family Fellowship (NTFF).

NTFF's congregation was primarily made up of Black Americans
and Nigerian, Haitian, and Jamaican immigrants. We were an intergenerational group of primarily working to lower middle-class folks navigating racism, classism, ableism, and redlining. These words mean real
things—like fervent prayer requests for medical debts to be absolved
and holding trunk parties to ensure parting college students had supplies
and love to go on. It meant pooling resources and sharing time.

This is important to note because we did not often have the lux-
ury of relying on the state, the medical industrial complex, or benev-
olent white folks for safety, security, or care. The reality was always
that we were to take care of each other. We did not call it accessibility
or access intimacy. In fact, I doubt we called it anything. However,

these concepts of mutual aid and collective care were evident in the norms that were shared.

Beloved elders became our "church mothers"—folks whose primary concern was the emotional and spiritual wellbeing of the church body itself. It was the collective responsibility of the parishioners to ensure that the needs of their body were taken care of before, during, and after our service time together.

> *"Who's going to pick up Mother Lois before church? Get there a little early. She likes to get to Bible school in the morning."*

> *"Who's taking Sister Mercy home after church this week? Her hip is hurting bad so we need someone that can take her down the ramp and help her in the wheelchair lift at home."*

I'm not sure whether church elders ever asked for formal accommodations, but it wasn't their primary or individual responsibility to do so. The community ethic held that their presence and wisdom should be honored. Honoring their wisdom in the space meant making sure their physical body could be in the space comfortably. This meant living in the pragmatics of listening, being flexible, and being responsive.

This church was generally under-resourced, as is the case for many small Black churches of its type. So, folks needed to get creative. Ushers saved the front-row seats for parishioners who were Deaf and an associate pastor was always assigned to sit directly opposite for lipreading. Parishioners learned basic signs and folks would offer transcription in between (of the pen and paper variety). Folks used whatever they had: the backs of service programs, tithing envelopes, etc.

The ethic of access intimacy was in the flow of service, communicated across the pulpit in simple ways:

> *"We'll wait for everybody to get to the text. Ushers are moving around to assist those who may want or need it…"*

"Feel free to move out into the aisles…"

"I'll say that again…"

* * *

Ultimately, I can't tell you how best to organize for your specific congregation. But that's not my work. It's yours to carry on from here. It might look like slowing down, reallocating resources, breaking traditional formats of service, picking up people's medicines, pitching in to a care fund, consulting with LGBTQIA+ Black, Brown, and Indigenous disabled folx during sermon prep (and offering reciprocity and compensation). The principles of disability justice have a powerful potential to share our lives on an individual, interpersonal level, and systemic level. It only does that if we put them into practice. I'm clear that the way forward must include a communal ethic of care, the regular and consistent centering of folks' access needs, and the deconstruction of any institutions or institutional norms which insist that we view care as a private or individual matter. The just future that we imagine depends on this.

BIBLE BLUEPRINT: Luke 5:17–26

One of the stories that I enjoy is where the friends of a Bible character read as disabled cut open the roof in order to lower their friend down to Jesus. It's such a good example of access intimacy and collective care—even before Jesus "heals" him.—*Jade Perry*

Notes

1. Alice Wong, ed., *Disability Visibility: First-Person Stories from the Twenty-First Century* (New York: Vintage, 2020).

2. Tema Okun, "White Supremacy Culture: Coming Home to Who We Really Are," https://www.whitesupremacyculture.info/.

3. Johanna Hedva, "Sick Woman Theory," Mask Magazine, January 2016. Also here: https://johannahedva.com/SickWomanTheory_Hedva_2020.pdf.

4. Eli Clare, *Brilliant Imperfection: Grappling with Cure* (Durham: Duke University Press, 2017). The portmanteau bodymind can be attributed to disability justice scholars such as Eli Clare. It holds the idea that our minds and bodies aren't separate entities. They are part and parcel of each other. The things that impact our minds impact our bodies and vice versa.

5. Daniel Wood, "As Pandemic Deaths Add Up, Racial Disparities Persist—And in Some Cases Worsen," NPR, September 23, 2020.

6. Audre Lorde, "Age, Race, Class and Sex: Women Redefining Difference," in *Sister Outsider* (New York: Penguin, 2020), 104–14.

7. Talila A. Lewis, "Ableism 2020: An Updated Definition," January 25, 2020, https://www.talilalewis.com/blog/ableism-2020-an-updated-definition.

8. Sins Invalid, *Skin, Tooth and Bone: A Disability Justice Primer*, (self-published, 2019), https://www.sinsinvalid.org/disability-justice-primer.

9. Jane Coaston, "The Intersectionality Wars: Meet Kimberlé Crenshaw," *Vox*, May 28, 2019, https://www.vox.com/the-highlight/2019/5/20/18542843/intersectionality-conservatism-law-race-gender-discrimination.

10. Sara Goering, "Rethinking Disability: The Social Model of Disability and Chronic Disease," Current Reviews in Musculoskeletal Medicine 8, no. 2 (2015): 134–38, doi: 10.1007/s12178-015-9273-z.

11. Ibid.

12. Leah Lakshmi Piepzna-Samarasinha, *Care Work : Dreaming Disability Justice* (La Vergne: Arsenal Pulp Press, 2018), 14.

13. Sins Invalid, *Skin, Tooth and Bone.*

14. Maria Godoy and Daniel Wood, "What Do Coronavirus Racial Disparities Look Like State by State?" NPR, May 30, 2020.

15. Samantha Artiga, Bradley Corallo, and Olivia Pham, "Racial Disparities in COVID-19: Key Findings from Available Data and Analysis," KFF, August 17, 2020, https://www.kff.org/racial-equity-and-health-policy/issue-brief/racial-disparities-covid-19-key-findings-available-data-analysis/.

16. Mia Mingus, "Access Intimacy: The Missing Link," *Leaving Evidence*, May 5, 2011, https://leavingevidence.wordpress.com/2011/05/05/access-intimacy-the-missing-link/.

17. Ashon T. Crawley, *BlackPentacostal Breath: The Aesthetics of Possibility* (New York: Fordham University Press, 2016), 26.

18. Ibid., 34.

6

. . .

DISMANTLING CHRISTIANITY FOR
INDIGENOUS SELF-DETERMINATION

. . .

SKY ROOSEVELT MORRIS

Indigenous Peoples begin with gratitude. It is imperative that I acknowledge the lands, ancestors, and all Life that sustains us in my gratitude. I have been fortunate enough to reside in Tabeguache Ute Nation territory for most of my life, and I write this paper from unceded Cheyenne and Arapahoe lands, known by many as the colonizer name Denver, Colorado. There were over forty-eight Indigenous Peoples and Nations who were connected to this part of Turtle Island home prior to invasion. The Indigenous Peoples of this place still remain in spite of the destructiveness of the colonizer world. Vine Deloria, Jr. reminds us that "as long as the descendants of those Nations and Peoples live on the land, and point to the places where their People's history was experienced, those Nations and Peoples will always exist."[1] May the Indigenous Life of all places continue to disrupt colonialism and thrive wherever possible, and may Indigeneity always be a living act of decolonization.[2]

In addition, none of what I will share in this piece would be possible without all those who have come before, who lived, and sacrificed so that we may still be here as Indigenous Peoples of Turtle Island. These are the contributions and collections of a brilliant and beautiful community of shapers, changers, creators, and resistors to which I belong and would be nothing without. I am forever grateful to my entire community, particularly to my mom and dad, my uncles Glenn and Russ, my Roosevelt relatives, my Morris relatives, my Locust relatives, my Means relatives, the American Indian Movement of Colorado, Four Winds American Indian Council, Tall Bull Memorial Grounds Council, the Denver Native community, and the countless relatives and friends along the way. Thank you to the Indigenous scholars and heroes such as Dr. Debra Harry, Sharon Venne, Steven Newcomb, Dr. Tamara Starblanket, Dr. tink tinker, Prof. Natsu Saito, Ward Churchill, Dr. Linda Tuhawi-Smith, Dr. Graham Smith, Moana Jackson, Drs. Nepia and Rangimarie Mahuika, Phyllis and Waste Win Young, and Red Fawn Janis for showing me the value of making our voices and presence radiate throughout spaces and times where anti-Indigeneity continually attempts to prey on our homelands and Peoples.

Giving voice and respect to the thousands of Indigenous children being uncovered outside the genocide schools in so-called Canada, as I write this chapter, is a fundamental responsibility that I possess as an Indigenous author. Each of the children were stolen and killed as a consequence of the worldview begun by Christian missionaries and in tandem with the invader-state (United States, Canada, Australia, New Zealand, etc.) policy.[3] This chapter is dedicated to all the Indigenous children stolen, murdered, found, missing, and those who somehow survived. May their rage and cries for justice fuel our unending perseverance to freedom.

When I started this endeavor to write about the suggested topic, "Indigenous Sovereignty," which is a term that I ultimately reject, for a collaborative project organized and funded by the United Church of Christ, and published by "Pilgrim" Press, I pondered for quite an extensive period what I, as an Indigenous woman, possibly could say to Christian denominations who have historically and presently both been the beneficiaries of the genocide and dispossession of Indigenous Peoples across the planet, and are instrumental in the creation and maintenance of the horrific colonial death culture that continues to actively prevent Indigenous Peoples from liberation and decolonization. What can possibly be shared about Indigenous self-determination with those who have been the greatest inhibitor of that birthright and aspiration?

Discussions of "truth and reconciliation" with Indigenous Peoples are common today. We cannot resolve or "reconcile" until the truth has been fully realized, told honestly, and publicly. "If we are to talk seriously about the necessity of liberation, we are talking about the destruction of the whole complex of Western theories of knowledge and the construction of a new and more comprehensive synthesis of human knowledge and experience."[4] In order for Indigenous liberation to be realized, the destruction of the Christian Doctrine of Discovery and Domination[5] in all of its forms and manifestations must also come to pass. Not simply the legal Doctrine of Discovery but the *worldview* that helped shape it must also be challenged and demolished. "For it is the manner in which people conceive reality that motivates them to behave in certain ways, that provides them with a system of values, and that enables them to behave in certain ways, and that enables them to justify their activities."[6]

There is still quite a lot to say regarding the violence perpetrated by religious institutions and invader-state governments against Indigenous Peoples, predominantly because this onslaught of violence has never ceased. Only through understanding and acknowledging the complex destructive manifestations of colonialism in Indigenous contexts can the invader world begin to grapple with the immense need for Indigenous Peoples' liberation. Colonization by invader-state governments has largely been enabled by collusion with religious ideologies and institutions. I am not convinced that one can take seriously the work of decolonization and self-determination and remain a part of an institution whose base assumption is that "[Christianity] sees others religions as foes rather than simply as different. It sees other traditions as inferior rather than as having their own integrity."[7] Tink Tinker writes, "Christian missionaries, of all denominations working among American Indian Nations, were partners in genocide."[8] However, Deloria reminds us that "whether we [Indigenous Peoples] like it or not we are inevitably tied to the fate of Western man who has invaded our lands and among whom we now dwell. When he falls we believe we shall still survive. But we know it will be at a terrible cost."[9]

My chapter is a fundamental, perhaps even an existential challenge to the Christians successors to the original invaders of the Americas. There have been extensive statements, books, speeches, art installations, interviews, panels, and overall discussions from Indigenous movers and thinkers such as Vine Deloria Jr., Steven Newcomb, tink tinker, Glenn Morris, and Tamara Starblanket,[10] among countless others who have clearly articulated the consistent genocidal conflict between the worldviews of Indigenous Peoples and the worldviews of Western Christian Euro-Americans. Although some small steps and gestures have been made, such as various Christian congregations repudiating the Christian Doctrine of Discovery and Domination, more radical structural transformations inevitably still need to take shape, such as giving land back to Indigenous Peoples. Deloria provides even greater clarity about the prerequisites for dismantling invader-state colonialism by challenging basic invader assumptions:[11]

- That time is uniform and continuous.

- That our species originated from a single source.

- That our descriptions of nature are absolute knowledge.

- That the world can be divided into subjective and objective.

- That our understanding of our species is homogenous.

- That by projection of present conditions we can understand human history, planetary history, or the universe.

- That inductive and deductive reasoning are the primary tools for gaining knowledge.

There is a particular lens that informs my work in this area, and that has greatly shaped my perspective on Christianity and its use as an instrument of colonization. My mother, a fierce and unwavering White Mountain N'dee woman, was stolen by Christian missionaries when she was very young, perhaps six years old, and was prohibited from seeing her homelands, family, or Nation again for nearly two decades. From the moment that those missionaries stole my mother, she was sentenced onto the slow death march that only colonization compels from Indigenous Peoples. A death march to erase her memory and identity as an N'dee woman, to give her amnesia about her spiritual connection to the Earth and to all the universe, and to beat from her consciousness that we as Indigenous Peoples still and always will have a birthright to freedom in our homeland. Through this lens, I embrace the late Vine Deloria's insights when he wrote, "Christianity is the chief evil ever to have been loosed on the planet."[12]

The demand for conscientious action—and not grandiose empty gestures that change little for Indigenous Life—comes from this place. Several Christian denominations have publicly repudiated the Christian Doctrine of Discovery and Domination. For example, the UCC did so in 2013, and the Episcopal church in 2009.[13] These efforts, while commendable, are insufficient to the ultimate aspirations of many Indigenous Peoples. Change is required on four levels: structural, institutional, community, and individual. How can these "change agents" remain immersed and surrounded by an ideology of invader-state colonialism that is rooted in white supremacist heteropatriarchy? There is no reforming institutions and ideologies that can only be sustained through the oppression and dismissal of other worlds and lifeways. As Audre Lorde once so eloquently put, "The master's tools will never dismantle the master's house. They may allow us temporarily to beat him at his own game, but they will never enable us to bring about genuine change."[14] To me, the futile attempts of "progressive" religious groups to reform and rebrand themselves to falsely appear inclusive of Indigenous and all people who are being oppressed is equally harmful.

Inclusivity in this sense means that colonialism is doing its job. When I see Indigenous missionaries, I do not feel as though these two opposing worldviews are coming together in an intentional and meaningful way, but rather that colonization has taken hold of an Indigenous person, most likely an entire community, and caused them to betray a key piece of their Indigeneity. This colonial process is using them to promote the same old colonial genocidal project on anything deemed "other," most likely other Indigenous Peoples—sometimes their own family and friends.

When I think of Indigenous self-determination, the word sovereignty is nowhere in my strategic design. European frameworks of nation-state sovereignty have no place in Indigenous thought or language. Sovereignty is a term coined by invader states for the sole benefit of invader states. Sovereignty first appears in the works of Jean Bodin, inspired by Nicolo Machiavelli, and later Hobbes elaborates on the concept. Sovereignty is about the state having a monopoly on the legitimate use of violence in order to protect itself and its interests. This kind of system requires coercion, hierarchical structures, and the perception that humanity is innately bad.[15] This is reiterated through Christian doctrine in that it views nature as evil or at best neutral; the universe is dead, except for man; and that the human experience is always an adversarial situation.[16] Similar to the political philosophy of sovereignty, "the central doctrine of Christianity suggests that the human being is guilty of a cosmic sin simply by virtue of being human."[17]

Taiaiake Alfred suggests that the European notion of sovereignty is in "direct opposition with Indigenous worldviews, which have no absolute authority, no coercive enforcement of decisions, no hierarchy, and no separate ruling entity."[18] The reason that Indigenous Peoples of Turtle Island use the word "sovereignty" was due to the political environment of the 1970s, which was talking about the international character of Indigenous Peoples, who at the time were demanding their rightful place at the United Nations.[19] However, reexamining the colonizing roots of the word and the components necessary to meet the definition, more meaningful and accurate language should be utilized. When we, as Indigenous Peoples, discuss this work we discuss it as Indigenous self-determination, Indigenous freedom, Indigenous liberation, Indigenous independence from the invader state, which are all more appropriate descriptions of what I am trying to convey.

Indigenous self-determination is beautifully shared in a panel discussion by Shareena Clanton of the Wangatha, Yamatji, Noongar, and Gidja Peoples of Australia: "we [Indigenous Peoples] want to be the authors of our own destinies, we want to be the voice."[20] The idea is simple but profound. In the international community, it has formulated as such:

> In its essence, the right of self-determination means that individuals and peoples should be in control of their destinies and should be able to live out their identities, whether within the boundaries of existing States or through independence. More than an outcome, self-determination should be seen as a process subject to revision and adjustment, and its outcome must correspond to the free and voluntary choice of

the peoples concerned, within a framework of human rights protection and non-discrimination. Self-determination cannot be understood as a one time choice, nor does it extinguish with lapse of time because, like the rights to life, freedom and identity, it is too fundamental to be waived. As an ongoing democratic exercise, self-determination entails a people's equal participation in decision making, a continuous dialogue by virtue of which parties adjust and readjust their relationship for mutual benefit.[21]

Lenape scholar Steven Newcomb encourages Indigenous Peoples to "exercise our self-determination on a daily basis: through our personal lives, our professional lives, our family lives, our community lives, our ceremonial lives, and through the reaffirmation of the continuing existence of our respective Indigenous Nations."[22] Indigenous self-determination is to live freely in your ancestral lands, to not become a missing and or murdered Indigenous person, to not take your life before you've even begun to live; it is to create worlds and futures beyond the confines of colonialism, it is to speak your language, it is to take all of the responsibilities that true freedom encompasses. Through this perspective, Indigenous self-determination does not need to be "saved" by Christians, Christians simply need to dismantle the institutions of colonialism and racism they participate in and uplift, and to leave Indigenous Peoples alone to again "be the authors of our own destinies."

Vine Deloria once said that, "If we [Indigenous Peoples and Nations] change the way that Western people think, the way they collect data, which data they gather, and how they arrange that information, then we are truly speaking of liberation."[23] My position is that s does not fall on the shoulders of Indigenous Peoples to help facilitate the change in invader society, but it falls to invaders themselves to begin doing this work. In place of flocking to every reservation and urban Indian enclave to spread the "good word," instead spread the "decolonial word" amongst your own congregation and community. The Indigenous world cannot handle any more thieves, appropriators, liars, or colonizers if we want any world to find a home in the future. "It is not merely for the sake of humans that we must shift away from the 'subdue' and 'dominion' mentality and behaviors traced to the Old Testament and ancient Christendom. We must also do so for the sake of all living things, including Mother Earth and our future generations. As the Original Nations and Peoples of Great Turtle Island, we must invite the world to walk with us on this beautiful path of life in keeping with a central teaching of Indigenous law: Respect the Earth as our Mother, and Have a Sacred Regard for All Living Things."24

Colonization will not succeed. There is too much positivity, resistance, and beauty in the world to let something as greedy, ugly, and unquenchable as colonialism take out Indigenous Life and all of Life. Colonization will not steal our right to be free with our Homelands, Peoples, and Nations. I know these things because of my mother. Despite the endless colonizer violence thrown upon my mother, a piece of her remained N'dee into her journey to the ancestors. There are very few things, like hope and place, that we as Indigenous Peoples still get to hold onto in a world that is becoming more and more unrecognizable and unlivable for Indigenous life. The glimmer of our ancestors that would come through my mother, in her words, actions, tears for the sacred mountains and the heartbeat of the Earth, her love for my dad and me, her love and unconditional pride to be N'dee: those are the moments that I reflect on and know that colonization did not steal my mother away completely. A piece of my mother will always belong to the freedom of this land, of our N'dee Peoples, of all Indigenous Peoples, of the universe and all that are fulfilling their responsibilities within it. "In that [piece], we are free. A [piece], it is small, and it is fragile, and it is the only thing in the world worth having. We must never lose it or give it away. We must never let the [colonizers] take it from us,"[25] because that is the very essence of who we are as Indigenous Peoples, free.

> *Only one thing is sadder than remembering that you were once free, and that's forgetting that you were once free. That would be the saddest thing of all. That's one thing we Indians will never do.*

—Noble Red Man (Matthew King), Oglala Lakota elder[26]

BIBLE BLUEPRINT: Book of Joshua, Matthew 28:19

The Bible has been used to justify colonization and Indigenous genocide, whether via outright murder or genocide via forced assimilation and loss of culture. See for example the book of Joshua, or Matthew 28:19. We encourage you to read scripture with honesty about the harm that we have perpetrated with it, and to make reparations to indigenous folks such as giving land back, as Sky describes in this chapter. —*Anne Dunlap*

Notes

1. Vine Deloria, *For This Land: Writings on Religion in America* (New York: Routledge, 1999), 272.

2. Leanne Betasamosake Simpson, *As We Have Always Done: Indigenous Freedom Through Radical Resistance* (Minneapolis: University of Minnesota Press, 2017).

3. George E. Tinker, *Missionary Conquest: The Gospel and Native American Cultural Genocide* (Minneapolis: Augsburg Fortress, 1993), 4.

4. Deloria, *For This Land*, 106.

5. Steven T. Newcomb, *Pagans in the Promised Land* (Golden, CO: Fulcrum Publishing, 2008).

6. Deloria, *For This Land*, 106. See also Vine Deloria, *God is Red* (Golden, CO: Fulcrum Publishing, 1994).

7. Deloria, *For This Land*, 145.

8. Tinker, *Missionary Conquest*, 4.

9. Deloria, *For This Land*, 80.

10. Tamara Starblanket, *Suffer the Little Children: Genocide, Indigenous Nations, and the Canadian State* (Atlanta: Clarity Press, 2018).

11. Deloria, *For This Land*, 107.

12. Ibid., 146.

13. See "Repudiations by Faith Communities,"Doctrine of Discovery, July 20, 2021, https://doctrineofdiscovery.org/faith-communities/; United Church of Christ, "The Repudiation of the Doctrine of Discovery: A Biblical Reflection," https://www.ucc.org/what-we-do/justice-local-church-ministries/justice/faithful-action-ministries/racial-justice/justice_racism_doctrine-of-discovery/; The Episcopal Church, "Repudiation of the Doctrine of Discovery," https://www.episcopal church.org/indigenousministries/repudiation-of-the-doctrine-of-discovery/.

14. Lorde, "The Master's Tools Will Never Dismantle the Master's House."

15. Glenn T. Morris, "Vine Deloria, Jr., and the Development of a Decolonizing Critique of Indigenous Peoples and International Relations," in Native Voices: American Indian Identity and Resistance, ed. Richard A. Grounds, George E. Tinker, and David E. Wilkins (Lawrence: University Press of Kansas, 2003), 97–154.

16. Deloria, *For This Land*, 147–51.

17. Ibid., 156.

18. Taiaike Alfred, *Peace, Power, Righteousness: An Indigenous Manifesto*, New York: Oxford University Press, 1999), 55–57.

19. Morris, "Vine Deloria, Jr.," 97–154.

20. Shareena Clanton, "Q&A: Shareena Clanton Says Indigenous People Want to Be 'the author of our own destinies,'" YouTube video, 10:31, February 19, 2018, https://www.youtube.com/watch?v=FghAgcOZgUg.

21. Alfred-Maurice de Zayas, *Interim Report of the Independent Expert on the Promotion of a Democratic and Equitable International Order* (Geneva: United Nations, 2014).

22. Newcomb, *Pagans in the Promised Land*, 159.

23. Deloria, *For This Land*, 106.

24. Newcomb, *Pagans in the Promised Land*, 165.

25. *V for Vendetta*, dir. James McTeigue (2005; Los Angeles: Silver Pictures), film.

26. Harvey Arden, *Noble Red Man: Lakota Wisdomkeeper Matthew King* (Hillsboro, OR: Beyond Words Publishing, 1994), Page?

7

. . .

BUILDING A JUST ECONOMY

. . .

Sᴇᴋɪɴᴀʜ Hᴀᴍʟɪɴ

REFLECTION

Why do I do this work? Because I am my ancestors' dream as my kids are mine. Because I am created to help recreate this world into a just economy and world for all. Because as I endeavor to be a disciple or follower of Jesus, my soul cannot rest until all are free. Because I am a Black Southern mom living in America.

Perhaps the better question is, how have I learned to do this work on my journey? 1 John 3:18 states, "Little children, let us love, not in word or speech, but in truth and action." What does that mean for a Black pastor of a white, rural, evangelical church? A church whose members do not know racism as a system of oppression based on race but rather know racism by its incorrect definition of prejudice and bigotry? If the *imago dei* is truly made flesh in us and we live into that calling, then we must love and show love. Love is about understanding and accountability. In that white, rural church, love means accountability to my parishioners' humanity, despite our differences. It means not approaching my ministry with a sense of supremacy because of what I know and they don't, but leading as a servant, understanding that we are both moved by the deep human yearning to see our kids grow up and prosper. I had to learn how to turn this abstract love into accountable action when it came time for an evangelism outreach event called the "Wild Game Dinner."

The year I came to pastor, the church went all out for their annual "Wild Game Dinner" with a Christian band, kids games, wild game (of course), and even prizes from local businesses. The Elder in charge was so excited to tell me that this year's raffle prizes would be muzzle-loaders, which are front-loading guns. This was less than a year after the Sandy Hook shooting. I was particularly disturbed by the idea that a church would give lethal weapons as a raffle gift after so many children had been killed. The Elder was disturbed that I would think something was wrong with a muzzleloader. I had to remember this is an area of the country where lots of families hunt as a rite of passage, as well as to simply put food on the table. One of our middle-schoolers even wore a camouflage dress to her first school dance.

With the prayers of the righteous literally from all over the country, we came to a compromise. Since a local spice company was a sponsor and attended the event to demonstrate how to process your own deer meat, we gave meat grinders as the raffle prizes. Families were able to learn how to process their own meat and have a meat grinder to take home. For families that hunted for food, it was a huge blessing. It also gave me an entry point to addressing food insecurity in a way that was culturally appropriate for the area. Those conversations led the church to revamp the food drives/offerings that it supported and to cultivate a partnership with Bread for the World, which started them on the road from charity to justice (see chapter 14 on mutual aid).

I learned that even though cultural norms can vary widely within the church, our shared human needs still tie us together. It is through

these needs—talking about them and following them to their roots—
that people begin to move from private charity to public activism.

WHAT IS ECONOMIC JUSTICE?

At its core, economic justice is about making sure all people have the
resources they need to thrive: food, shelter, health care, support. But
so often, because of the way we've organized affairs in our woefully
limited human wisdom, people go without these basic needs. As people of God, we must never forget that the world is made up of our siblings—people like us who God created in their image, and who God
loves unconditionally. As God called Ezekiel, so our God calls us as
witnesses to God's promise: to prophesy breath into the dry bones of
a broken economy through our advocacy and actions, so that through
us God can breathe fresh life and abundance.

In the lives of our churches, likewise, we must breathe life into
those who are struggling, for as the apostle says, "how does God's love
abide in anyone who has the world's goods and sees a [sibling] in need
and yet refuses help?" (1 John 3:17) Thus, in the life of the church,
charity and justice must go hand in hand. As people of Christ, citizens
of the Kin-dom of God, we must witness and prophesy to those who
cannot yet see, through our acts of love in our communities and our
fierce struggle for a just economy in our world.

Just economic relations touch more than money. The economy,
rightly considered, includes the land, plants, and animals, as well as
other human beings. Beginning in the colonial era, colonization
teaches us to treat the land as a lifeless stockpile made for us to extract
wealth and resources with impunity. With the advent of climate
change and mass extinctions, we can no longer ignore the fact that
our thoughtless extraction has deadly consequences. However, as people in the economic habit of extraction, we are often guilty of treating
human beings in the same way we treat the land. From the recent

history of African and Indigenous enslavement to the modern abuse of laborers in all parts of the world today, many of our economic relationships are rooted in extracting profits from the labor of others, then ignoring the cries of those who aren't able to find housing or feed their children with the small wages that are given to them.

As people of God, we must reckon with the false idols of our current economic order, which perpetuates all kinds of human suffering, and turn instead to God's vision of right relations. After all, our God is a God of righteousness as well as love, a God who thunders support of the poor and the oppressed, who casts down the strong and the full and "lifts the needy from the ash heap to make them sit with princes" (1 Samuel 2:8). The question is: how can we, as people of faith, join God in this work? We, whose vision is so clouded by our assumptions of what is possible, need to turn to our Creator to dream God-given visions of what could and must be.

Turning to biblical witness, right economic relations have two wings: (1) reparation for past economic sins and forgiveness of debts to diminish the wealth gap, and (2) the creation of strong support networks to sustain the just distribution of resources going forward.

In Isaiah 58:12, God calls Israel's ruling elite to become "repairers of the breach" by doing justice to those they had previously oppressed: to "offer your food to the hungry and satisfy the needs of the afflicted." It's a lesson we teach our children—if you took your sister's crayons, first, you say you're sorry. Then, you give the crayons back. Reparations means repairing the breaches caused by the systems we have benefited from and participate in, be they white supremacy, colonialism, or patriarchy. What counts as "reparation" must be determined in conjunction with the wounded party and cannot be treated as charity. Reparations are justice.

In the Western world, reparations are not only a concern inside of our own communities, but also within the global context. Many "third-world" nations were underdeveloped and then abandoned by the Europeans and Americans who extracted wealth from the land and then left the people they enslaved or exploited to fend for themselves. The deadly cocktail of white supremacy, colonialism, and predatory capitalism has left many people of color in our global community in abject poverty without any hopes of economic mobility. This injustice has bred massive wealth gaps, health disparities, ecological devastation, and national debt crises in many of these young nations that are directly traceable to massive European and American disinvestment in their once settler-colonies. The struggles of these peoples are not "someone else's problem." They are our people, our problems.

Likewise, within the United States, we must understand that the unmanageable debt people accumulate throughout their lives, whether from student loans, medical bills, or consumer loans, is often tied to histories of oppression and wealth extraction. Instead of providing affordable education, medical care, and personal necessities, our economic structures have demanded that poor folks take out loans to "afford" necessities we have made unaffordable, leading them into a cycle of debt that they cannot escape. Debt enslavement has been a problem since biblical times, which is why God ordained "sabbath years" every seven years and a "Year of Jubilee" in the fiftieth year (see Leviticus 25 and Deuteronomy 15), when all debts in Israel were to be cancelled and all debt-enslaved workers freed. Biblical debt jubilee, be it from old student loan debt, medical bills, or predatory payday loans, is something we should fight for in our communities and on a national scale. Poverty isn't something people earn, it's something that happens to them, and it's our job as Christians to help free them from the traps that our unjust economic structures have built and advocate that those traps be abolished.

Of course, even if we can manage to wipe the slate clean of past economic wrongs, we must also look to the future and put better systems in place so that all people can get equal access to the resources and care that they need to thrive. As Christians, we are meant to be a light to the world, bearers of God's Kin-Dom, who strive to recognize and respect the needs of all of God's children. The early church recognized this sacred duty materially as well as spiritually, as described in Acts 4:34–35, where "there was not a needy person among them, for as many as owned lands or houses sold them and brought the proceeds of what was sold. They laid it at the apostles' feet, and it was distributed to each as any had need." At least in the church, we ought to recognize that the resources we possess are a gift of God for all, not just for ourselves and our families. We must fight the dual messages of greed and scarcity that plague our society and advocate for policies that flow from the true abundance of God's provision.

In that vein, churches can advocate for strong social safety nets supported by just taxation and champion local and national efforts to deliver medical care for all, food security, shelter, and care for children and the elderly. While private charity is a vital way for congregations to get hands-on experience with people in their communities in need of immediate help, such efforts must be bolstered by a broader justice vision and advocacy to create better public systems, so that those served might no longer be caught in the snares of hunger, homelessness, or neglect. Churches not on the frontlines of care can become involved in supporting labor organizing and worker's rights by advocating for fair wages, safe work conditions, and robust paid leave for all workers—including service and care workers (like waitresses and childcare providers) who have traditionally been left out of the gains of the labor movement. Grounded in the dignity of all human labor, such efforts would help ensure that those who do the difficult work of keeping our society functioning are given the respect, rest, and resources they need to live well.

As churches step into their calling as ministers prophesying God's economic justice to the dry bones of our society, they will be well-supported by keeping one foot planted in reparation and restorative justice movements and the other planted in advocacy for better safety nets and working conditions for all.

A VISION OF ECONOMIC JUSTICE

Where there is no vision, the people perish.
Proverbs 29:18 (KJV)

Then the Lord answered me and said: "Write the vision; make it plain on tablets, so that a runner may read it."
Habakkuk 2:2 (NRSV)

Vision. Such a simple word, yet it is often a challenge to actualize. Those of us who are visionaries are sometimes constricted or constrained by the pragmatic over the prophetic. We know what type of economy God has envisioned and shared in scripture, but it often seems like that will not easily or even realistically happen. Pragmatism has some organizer-advocates trapped in the framework of what can practically pass legislatively, or what we can do to mitigate the suffering of those in our midst, but what is practical cannot be the end of *our* work. The vision requires Ezekiel-style participation in the *re*-creation of the economy. Transformation and holy repair. We are called by God and God does not settle for the practical—our God is a God of miracles. Our job as the church is to make sure we put as much effort into advocating prophetically for this full vision of justice—even if it seems like it would require a miracle—as we do into revealing God's love through acts of local charity.

A simple area of ministry where vision is required to move from a "repair" or "charity" mindset to transformative change is food insecurity. Most churches have some type of ministry for people and families that are hungry, or food insecure. During the COVID-19 lockdown, many churches got involved in distributing groceries to families for the first time to assist those who had lost jobs and were in financial distress. I often think it simple, at least theoretically, to take someone from the charity ministry of food distribution, soup kitchens, and/or canned food drives to the justice work of recreating and transforming the food system in general (see chapter 14 on mutual aid).

However, when organizing in a congregation setting, it's important to understand that most people in the pews don't have the educational or theoretical resources to make the jump from charity to activism on their own. In general, most Americans receive cultural messaging that places individual responsibility at the core of their economic understanding. This means that most people have trouble fully understanding that systems often shape the economic options individuals can choose between—if they are given a choice at all. Because public schools do not teach any kind of systemic critical thinking (nor do many universities), the vast majority of Americans only learn about how economic systems function through outside searches, in community, and in our churches, if at all. We therefore should not be surprised or offended when the volunteers in our clothing closets, emergency assistance funds, homeless shelters, feeding ministries, etc., see the individuals and families facing these challenges as people who have made bad choices in their lives and are reaping the consequences of their choices.

We must instead realize our role as the church is not only to feed the hungry, but also to educate the misinformed so that we can step out together prophetically to advocate for God's justice. This process is not an easy one, nor is it quick. However, it is vital to stay faithful to God's call, and God provides a way if we are only willing to grasp it. I've found the way often arises for churches in the complexity uncovered in local charity work. For example, the opportunity for education and transformation presented itself to my local church in the form of a defunded feeding charity ministry while I was part of a pastoral team.

Our congregation for years had a ministry that fed healthy meals to individuals and families weekly in partnership with the local hospital. The hospital was given access to those coming to the church in need of a meal and they provided access to health education and healthcare through the dissemination of vaccines such as flu shots — even the COVID-19 vaccine. The hospital provided all the funding for the ministry because the pastor at the time the charity began was a member of the hospital board and it was a win-win for both the hospital and the church. However, when that pastor went on to other ministries and the hospital was about to merge with another one, the board decided that it would be a great time to reallocate resources. While it seemed like the end of the program, I recognized that the challenge was actually an opportunity to transform the feeding ministry into a new, expanded ministry of advocacy for the hungry aimed at disrupting a food system of oppression in order to transform it into one of liberation.

We knew we already had the elements of a successful advocacy ministry in the Message and a Meal feeding ministry — we just had to find a way for those struggling under the injustice of the food system to speak their experience and be heard. A key part of the transformation from charity to advocacy was asking guests to write down their prayer concerns each week. After all, prayer is protest. I learned this viscerally when, in a direct action at the US capitol in support of underpaid cafeteria workers, a guard told us that the prayers we were praying on the steps of the building were considered a protest action and charged us with illegally trespassing.

Thus, the prayer requests of those guests who were experiencing food insecurity were already what we needed to take with us to our state legislature, as well as to the US capitol, as evidence of how the system is not working for God's people. Those prayers — those pleas for help, in which our guests asked us to pray for them to find housing, to not have to come back next week because they were hungry, to find the mental health counselor they needed, or even a safe place to stay where they would not have to deal with rape or violence—were the evidence we needed to place at the foot of the legislature and say boldly "this has to end." The impacted community naming their prayers led to a realization that the ministry leadership did not have a sufficient power analysis to understand the systemic and structural issues people were facing. So first, we also needed to connect the leaders of the feeding ministry to the notion that this kind of prayer-advocacy is powerful and necessary—a means to disrupt the system of oppression that continues to plague the community they serve.

I quickly learned that the leadership of our feeding ministry did not rightfully understand systems and thus thought we prayer-advocates were making an undue ask of them. A transformation in ministry from charity to justice cannot occur if only the pastor(s) understand it. I recognized we needed to retrain and reeducate to these leaders to deconstruct the models and theologies that held them back so that we could take advantage of the opportunity to grow this ministry. Matthew 25 served as the rubric for our efforts, as well as a commitment to dismantling racism and eradicating systemic poverty. We found space for this education by partnering with a new ministry of the church that had arisen independently: the social justice advocacy ministry. The social justice advocacy ministry had formed as a voting initiative during the last election cycle; the ministry highlighted and brought together Black and Brown women who then led the way for their white sisters to join in the movement. After the election, the ministry was transformed into an educational initiative. The educational initiative had the goal of keeping members educated and engaged so that, at the appropriate time, they could be activated for change.

One of the first panel discussions we held was around food insecurity. We made sure to structure the training such that those providing resources and education were ones that understood that the food justice system needed to be transformed in and of itself. Our panel included professors from our historically Black colleges, Black farmers, and ministries that represented and advocated for food for all. We also discussed the connection between the theft of land from Black farmers and continued discrimination as it relates to access to resources of the United States Department of Agriculture, emphasizing how that all played a role in a food system that did not serve historically marginalized communities.

From this panel grew a hunger in the church to do more than simply serve—it was time to act. While some ministry leaders remained solely motivated to find funding to continue the charity ministry of feeding, many others wanted not only to continue the feeding ministry, but also to make sure that we worked ourselves out of a need of a feeding ministry at all. I would be remiss if I didn't mention the sage advice and wisdom of long-serving pastors and faith leaders who reminded us that one must care for each side in the work of charity and justice—there's no movement if the cars of a train aren't all joined together. That means our next step was to find people who could translate for the charity-focused leaders and the justice-focused leaders and to bring them all to a corporate table where all are welcome and feel empowered. To find these bridge builders required a clear assessment and discernment of the skills, gifts, and ministry potential of all volunteers and leaders. People who could understand the link between charity and justice were intentionally and strategically placed on each ministry so that the radical vision we had cultivated during our social justice training would continue guiding these ministries, whether or not pastoral leadership changes happened in the future.

The feeding ministry is still in the midst of transforming as I write this. As usual, the vision of a ministry takes much effort and time to actualize and to set in place. Currently, we are in the process of sharpening our lay ministers' social analysis and have planned our next regional educational event around food justice. In it, we will offer in-depth analysis of our food system's connection to Black farmers and their struggles to maintain their livelihood within racist systems, as well as to First Nations people and the histories of land theft and genocide that demand repair as a part of our bringing justice to those who work the land.

As our understanding of the economic systems that shape our world deepens, so does our motivation to remake those systems anew. By bringing together the love for those suffering nearest to us with the vision of God's justice, which demands more than individual remedies, we are driven to step out once again in faith, creatively and courageously bridging charity and advocacy to create a new model of life together. Though the road requires much wisdom and analysis, patience and listening, disagreement and prayer, who are we to strive for less? After all, we are a people called to live "in assurance of things hoped for and conviction of things not yet seen" (Hebrews 11:1).

BIBLE BLUEPRINT: 1 John 3:17, Leviticus 25, Deuteronomy 15, James 1:14–17

As people of faith, we are directed to come to the aid of people as siblings and neighbors, interpersonally and systemically, with charity and justice. Not either/or but both/and. These scriptures describe impacting lives by impacting economic systems. Let us be a part of ushering in "holy repair" of our economic system for a re-creation of our economy. —*Vahisha Hasan*

8

. . .

HEALING SUSTAINS OUR ORGANIZING

. . .

Teresa Mateus and Vahisha Hasan

Healing as a journey is as complicated and different as each person's personal trauma. There is no right way to heal and there is no certitude about what healing means for each person. HEALING[1]: How, when, and if trauma recovery and healing occurs is as multifarious as there are practitioners treating and supporting folks working through the path towards healing.

We appreciate the viewpoint of Bernice Dimas, founder of Hood Herbalism, and her statement: "I also like to complicate the term 'healing' by recognizing how ableist it can be to assume that everyone can or wants to heal or that healing is an ending point of any process."[2] In this way, we acknowledge that healing is a process, one of re-membering and re-embodying joy, peace and gratitude — without being plagued by the re-experiencing of the past pains of trauma — even if these emotions only come in single moments at a time and with the understanding that healing is not a conclusion point on a map.

Healing is the journey of stitching back together what was fragmented by the suffering of trauma — in mind, body, and spirit. It is mending the soul by way of learning how to be in healthy relationship with self and others. Depending on the intensity, duration, and time of onset in a lifetime of trauma(s) as well as a person's social location and identities, healing can be a process of returning to a healthy way of being or learning one for the first time. Depending on all these factors and others, it can be a journey of a moment in time or the work of a lifetime. We hold no judgment of what that path looks like and honor the fact that healing is also a choice — and the autonomy to choose not to heal is not one that should be shamed. Healers embrace the role of walking alongside those who have been impacted and wounded and support their needs in that moment, regardless of their choice or capacity to heal or not.

* * *

Teresa: I can remember as early as my teen years that people gravitated to a nameless something in me, an invisible resonance; they would come to me with their pain and their secrets, laying down their hurt at my feet like sacred offerings. Without qualification or certification beyond my own lived experience of hurt and annexation, I held the preciousness of others' stories: a story keeper for those who needed it, learning how to listen to really hear the pain of someone else.

Hearing stories, holding them as precious jewels, and seeing others in their pain wasn't a task I did or a job I applied for; it was just an essential essence of my being, as close as I could imagine a calling to be: something innate, seeking me more than me seeking it. It just was.

Because holding others' stories was as essential to me as breathing, for most of my growing years I never really considered healing as work per se; I always thought I would be a writer, a storyteller. Not until my own struggles with sexual assault and subsequent capital "T" trauma response and PTSD in my late teens, and my evolution over six years of seeking healing for my own pain, did I even begin to consider supporting healing for others as part of my professional calling.

Through my own trauma recovery and investment into emotional wellness for others, and through my time in graduate school for clinical social work, I knew I wanted my work to involve investing in the care of trauma survivors. That was always clear. The path of where that work flowed was never in my own plan; as the best, most important things often come, the river wound in its own way, pulling me into a current that I couldn't have dictated or directed if I wanted to.

While at New York University, I was assigned to be an intern at the Vet Centers doing readjustment counseling for combat veterans and survivors of military sexual trauma. This work offered me a way to actively serve, to do the work of intense trauma healing care, and also to find a space of nuance and compassion for those who served in war. War is an existential wound that rips at the soul, the healing of which is an existential process of return. I am grateful and honored to have done that work over the course of nearly a decade, which also prepared me for the next unexpected call, into the work of trauma healing for social movements.

Because of my trauma work, I found myself being called more frequently into faith-rooted, spiritual, and/or secular movement spaces. I realized that not only was there a cavernous space of hurt in movement—individual and collective—but also that the hurt came closest, in my experience, to embodying the unique characteristics of war trauma. This said a lot about the intensity of trauma in movement space; it also meant that in this unexpected, bizarre way, I had been uniquely equipped to support healing of trauma in movement space.

Over time I learned that while I don't organize *actions* in the movement, I have been called to organize *healers* for social movements. I found myself needing to think beyond my own individual work to support social movements and consider, from a macro level, how to organize and mobilize a larger contingent of healers around the country to respond to the rising need.

Out of that came the collaborative work with Vahisha and others to both offer the grassroots groundwork of healing care and also to equip a substantial contingent of healers to provide care, across a continuum of care from pastoral care providers, chaplains, ancestral and indigenous healers, medical and mental health clinicians, to naturopathic and body healers. There are times when movements feel like a warzone; as such, we need an organized and equipped force of healers to respond.

* * *

Vahisha: My personal foundations in healing began as a very excited little Black girl in a pink leotard and tights. At five years old, I delved into tap, jazz, and ballet in the studio, finding a way to move energy, expressing myself with my whole bodied self in a way I had not previously found in writing, music, nature, or even my first love, books. The yearly recitals were epic, formative, and planted some amazing seeds of what was possible in my body.

In Charlotte in my preteen years, a young Black woman named Noni Olanian taught me African-inspired dance at the Afro American Children's Theater (AACT) summer camps founded by Black women: Barbara Ferguson, Karen Jones Meadows, Ruth Sloane, Doris Frazier, and Margarette Freeman. In this communal setting, we learned through plays and other artistic expressions. The content of the plays, the lyrics of the songs, and the origins of the dance moves were connected to who we were, are, and will be as descendants of Africans. My soul was drawn to motion as a pathway to healing as well as to connecting to a stirring and powerful ancient something I couldn't name or see but knew I felt, knew was present in and through me.

Dance was healing me from what I experienced every day outside of my very loving home with my very loving, supportive, and fierce mommy. Healing was dancing alongside Black folks to drumbeats when I needed to move the energy of being called a hoodlum and dismissed as a foretold statistic of teen pregnancy, poverty, and crime based on my mom not being married. At eleven years old, healing for me was learning the motions of expressing appreciation for the land that brought forth the harvest; of moving the energy of daily racialized battles of worthiness determined by Eurocentric standards of capitalistic societal production. Healing became dancing to metabolize the questions, horror, and grief when Noni transitioned from this world at the hands of her husband after she left the marriage to escape abuse. Healing became dancing to metabolize my cousin Velvet's death, after she left that abusive relationship, taken from this earth by her ex-boyfriend on the eve of her college graduation.

During my undergraduate studies at the University of North Carolina, Chapel Hill I danced with Opeyo, a division of the Black Student Movement (BSM). Dancing reached another depth for me when, shortly after joining the Park Ministries[3] in Charlotte, I began liturgical dance, which offered a spiritual connection similar to what I previously experienced with African-inspired dancing. I was later blessed with the opportunity to choreograph for and lead the Judah Liturgical Dance Ministry at Second Calvary Baptist Church, where creating the movements that expressed the spirit of the songs and integrating the gifts and personality of the dancers became an unexpected pathway to healing. I experienced generations of Black people freely dancing together as an expression of love for God and each other, dancing through and to all that life brings, its valleys and mountain tops.

I've danced through miscarriages, a divorce, and family loss. I've danced to being an honor student in grad school after being a hot mess student in undergrad: five years of a dual masters degree program, where I began formalizing my relationship between faith and healing, divinity and mental health counseling. I danced to meeting my people in a gathering for community organizing in Atlanta known as Project South. During the Charlotte Uprising—a community response of outrage about the murder of Keith Lamont Scott by a Charlotte police officer—I was shown dancing on the news in Romare Bearden Park. Many texted and called, sarcastically asking if I was protesting or having a party. I was dancing in a park named after a Black creative in the midst of beloved community surrounded by militarized police. I was healing *in* and *as* my protest. I danced to job opportunities and churches that valued my gifts. I danced to my ordination under a Black woman, Rev. Dr. Gina Stewart, who said she was ordaining in public what God had already placed in me in private. I have danced through and to so much, y'all. Dances seen and unseen. I am still dancing, much slower, with much more body pain, and much less core strength. I am still healing.

Teresa and I met in 2016, on our paths to healing in different ways from similar life experiences. We connected in the importance of healing and in the necessity to include the dynamics of being in melanated bodies, traumatized by general life experiences as well as racialized experiences. We both were invited into communities during times of racial unrest and resistance to share knowledge and techniques of healing pathways. When I was called to Highlander Research and Education Center to create healing space for staff after a white supremacist burned down one of their offices, I consulted with Teresa on the drive, inquiring about the specifics of fire as a type of trauma and violence. From there, part of our shared work became how to curate healing spaces in community and coalition, rather than in less safe and unsustainable silos.

We impart to all of you that while we all need our own individual pathways to healing, healing work is also communal work. Organize yourselves in communities of healing that support each other as activists and liberators, fighting for positive social change and collective freedom.

INTENTIONALITY IN HEALING FOR ORGANIZERS

Social justice organizing is actually healing work. We are healing ourselves as we are healing the systems that harm. Movement healing is unique, based on the community of movement, the function and intention of movement, and who is showing up to do this work and how their lived experience of their own past pain informs their social change efforts. We affirm what you hear throughout this book: Organizing as a congregation *is* movement work. Church folks are not some separate entity apart from movement. There are many pathways to collective freedom and justice; organizing within a congregational context for these same goals places you firmly under the umbrella of movement. I, Vahisha, am often annoyed that when making introductions, I feel the need to name that I do faith, healing, and justice work in the world. I often ask aloud, "Who separated those concepts for us, and who does that serve for them to be considered separate?" Jesus certainly did not set such a dissecting example. To be clear, not all movement folks are nor need to be church folks. Not all church folks are going to be movement folks. But y'all church folks who are intentionally, actively organizing for justice and liberation, you *are* movement folks! Congregational organizing *is* movement work.

So, breathe and buckle up! Movement speaks to the ongoing, cyclical flow of organizing for change and resisting oppressive forces; it also includes specific campaigns, planned direct actions that address specific issues, or unplanned uprisings/responses to a particular event. So first receive that: this is ongoing work that can sometimes feel as if it lacks a defined beginning or ending, and your congregation will experience some waves in organizing. The good news is some of the fluctuations are predictable; you can prepare hearts, minds, and healing practices.

Perhaps within your congregation, you already have people gifted, called, and equipped in healing practices. That is an amazing benefit! And, we have found in our movement healing work that there are many well-equipped and well-trained folks, some with extensive clinical knowledge of trauma, who show up on the frontlines of movement expecting their existing skill sets and knowledge to translate in the moment without any additional knowledge or context-specific modifications.

There is, of course, good wisdom that does translate over, but not without preparation and accommodation for the uniqueness of the space. As a general framework, folks trained in clinical healing settings rarely have training or background in social movements; they come in unprepared to understand how movements work, or how to engage their healing work in that space. As a result, these well-intentioned professionals with much-needed skills never get fully integrated into the community, so some clinical needs for trauma healing in movement do not get met. In the same way, you may already have a base understanding and experience in organizing because some of those aspects are a built in part of church culture, you may have an excellent base understanding and experience in healing. What we offer is a way to coalesce that desire to integrate healing experience into this context of social movement.

UNDERSTANDING & ADDRESSING TRAUMA

Something that happened too much, too soon, too fast, or too long without something that was reparative.

—Resmaa Menakem on trauma[4]

Trauma manifests in hundreds of ways that are particular to each person and each lived experience. We consistently tell people that it is not fruitful to compare your trauma to someone else's. We cannot measure the validity or extremity of your lived experience by looking at someone else's; your trauma is no less true because you look at someone else's and deem theirs worse.

Post-traumatic stress disorder (PTSD) is trauma that gets stuck. When we experience something stressful, sometimes we move on from it; we acknowledge it was stressful-and maybe even experience some stress responses (panic, fear, etc.) right after the experience, but then we integrate it as past experience, moving on to the next thing. But sometimes that state of pain and fear doesn't get integrated into our memory effectively as a past experience and continues to feel as though it were ongoing in the present; that experience in our mind and body is constantly moved back into an active state of distress, as if we are in present danger again and again. The trauma gets stuck; we can't move on from it.

The closer in time to the incident of distress healers can help someone process the experience, the more likely someone will not become stuck. Healing modalities such as grounding and calming exercises, conversation about the incident or issue, music or motion, somatics, and so many more can support the impacted person integrating that experience as past, rather than present danger.

Therefore, it's important we build an infrastructure of layered care in our movement work. Layered care includes genuine connections and community, a diversity of healing modalities over time, and access to those modalities before, during, and after what would be considered high stress moments in movement. Layered care ensures activists and organizers have the support needed in moments of high stress so that they can avoid the eruption of new "stuck trauma", and that care holds us through the long haul of ongoing healing of our individual stories and experiences of pain and hurt.

Pre/Peri/Post Movement Stress: Traumatic Experiences in Movement

Recognizing there is a flow of movement that includes a flow of healing is how healing becomes an integrated part of justice work. Healing should not be seen as an individual or even communal activity that you check off and consider done. "I did the grounding" or "we did the processing that one time after the hard thing" is not integrated healing. Integrated, layered healing in movement is an opportunity to receive and reciprocate healing as we heal these harmful systems, not just reaching for the healing after we are specifically impacted and realize we need healing. We always need healing and healing should always be available.

* * *

BREATH FLOW
*Inhale with intention, preparing the body
for the being/moving/doing.
Take in what you need.*

* * *

Pre-Movement Stress: Trauma was present before every rendition of movement. Present in the bodies of our ancestors. Present in our own bodies. We bring that trauma to our churches and to our efforts toward social change. In the same way white supremacy was present before the murders of Trayvon Martin and Breonna Taylor, trauma was present before a particular horror or injustice moved you to act. Put healing infrastructure in place prior to the next violent taking of a Black life, separation of families, criminalization of access to resources, and continued colonization of absolutely everything. We can't always predict *when* new horrors *will* happen, but we do know they will happen, and there are freedoms forever worth fighting for. This healing foundation will support your future organizing. So prior to any planned actions, as you are forming your congregational organizing identities, even as you wrestle with how and when to show up, integrate healing work into this "before" time. How you heal individually and collectively *before* the uprising, organizing campaign, or action will undergird how you heal through the waves to come.

* * *

BREATH FLOW
Intentionally hold the breath,
bringing awareness of the body in the present.
Notice the areas of goodness and tension.

* * *

Peri-Movement Stress: Rather than trying to avoid stress when actively doing social change work—especially because avoiding it isn't actually possible!—your congregation should expect to encounter and experience stress and evolving, unresolved trauma. This means you need to be *super gentle* with your own places of stress and trauma, *super gentle* in being aware of your tender places and the tender places of others, and *super gentle* in equipping yourselves to maintain relationships and community. *We need each other.* Stress and trauma can strain these very necessary human connections, and how we navigate the high stress times of movement deeply impacts how we relate to one another. Use the healing infrastructure you already have in place; then include other intentional supports *during* your increased stressed efforts to resist, organize, and mobilize that meet the increased need. This "during" moment is also the place of possibilities and potentially the precipice of change. This *eustress*, stress from a positive source, can be beautiful and binding. Lean into the goodness available even as stress abounds.

* * *

BREATH FLOW
Extend your exhale,
signaling the body to decompress.
Release back into the world what you don't need.

* * *

Post-Movement Stress: You made it through the thing! Honor that! Intentional healing infrastructure should continue *after* the direct action, uprising, or policy campaign. This requires that your healing efforts are as organized and mobilized as your actions toward social change. Healing is integral to and inseparable from what you conceive as organizing. Recovering from the high stress time is just as important as preparing for and navigating during the high stress time. Just as healing should not be considered optional, healing should also not be contingent on the outcome of the action, uprising, or policy campaign. The binary frameworks of winning and losing do not speak to the expansive needs of healing. Having strategized, planned, sacrificed something(s), poured out one's self, and labored on behalf of freedom, you need and deserve layered care—especially because, as we discussed in the beginning, movement is ongoing work.

CHARLOTTESVILLE, VA: MOVEMENT HEALING REFLECTIONS

We both have offered healing in many different spaces. We chose this shared healing space as an example of the strategizing, planning, collaboration, sacrifice, outpouring, and freedom laboring needed for layered care in a time of amazing organizing in the face of a violent threat. We share this story with you as a case study for your own action towards providing care for movements and organizers. Learnings take many paths. May our learning support your path.

August 2017

Teresa: I remember the weekend of the "unite the right" white supremacist rally very clearly. I had friends and colleagues there, both local clergy organizers in Charlottesville who had been organizing for months and folks who went to support them that weekend. They started gathering together earlier that week, preparing for the counterprotests which would happen simultaneously and in response to the blasphemy of white power chants which would inevitably fill the streets.

I was facilitating a workshop in Chicago on, ironically or timely (or both), healing for social movements. From our little nexus of the universe half the country away, the full weight of the evening didn't fully penetrate, but a chilling unease settled in the room where we gathered, filled with movement healers and organizers who know how quickly bad can move to worse in kerosene-laden moments like that one.

When things fully erupted, I was invited by folks on the ground to come provide healing support. I arrived in Charlottesville with one support person coming with me from Chicago. I showed up because I was asked, in relationship with folks on the ground; as a trauma provider who supports movement, gut instinct had me on a plane within twenty-four hours. There were so many lessons learned in what followed.

I was lucky to have a good team of folks already established on the ground, both local folks and folks from national organizing communities who were supporting local folks at their invitation. The Unitarian Universalists sent their national organizer to support; they were amazing, setting me up in a house donated by a family who was out of town, as well as with space at one of the local U.U. churches as a home base of care. I began assessing the community and needs and building a plan for triage and support. I set up drop-in hours at the U.U. office where folks could come see me during the day. In the evening, I would facilitate support circles where people came to share space with each other and to process what they experienced.

I was, in truth, exhausted and overwhelmed; without an infrastructure of other providers with me, I felt like I was existing in a silo of my own making, each night coming back to the house, tossing and turning as the stories of the day rumbled through my head and heart, getting up early every morning to go back and do it all again. The week I spent in Charlottesville taught me incalculable lessons, solidifying the flickers of truths I had only lightly leaned into before. The need for this work was great and felt unending. The existing capacity and infrastructure of support can be limited, and in areas of surging increased need, like Charlottesville, often insufficient on the ground. Additionally, I met numerous well-intentioned folks while in town — clergy, healers, community-members — who said with humility, still greatly impacted: "We want to help, but we just don't know how." This paved the way for the declarative clarity of what would become Trauma Response and Crisis Care for Movements (TRACC)[5] and our network: a space for healers who want to help but don't know how to engage in a movement context, or healers who want to partner with others in support of movement.

AUGUST 2018: ONE YEAR LATER

Vahisha: Teresa and I were invited to Charlottesville one year after khaki-wearing, tiki-torch-carrying white supremacists spewed hate and violence in an effort to retain what they saw as their superior position in the world. Along with several other women of color, we led a Service of Healing and Repair event in a local church for a community expressing loss, fear, shame, and a desire to connect. We covered the sanctuary space with colorful fabric that thematized water as a medium of healing. We offered a healing container, sharing space, music, dance, grounding exercises, poetry, intentions, and a communal water ritual. For some, this service was received as a healing experience.

We also wanted to ensure care was being provided to activists not desiring to come to a service in a church setting. So, we went to the colleges and the main area of activist and fascist/military presence. Walking past tanks and barricades, underneath the scope of snipers, we held space for those still doing frontline resistance against the violence of white supremacy. Teresa had consulted for some Charlottesville churches and clinicians throughout the year, so we went to where a church was organizing healing support services.

The setup was amazing! There were multiple floors of food and medical supplies, healers offering diverse healing modalities, arm bands that identified emotional support medics; someone from the congregation shared the story of the church leadership rejecting the police's request to use their roof for surveillance and snipers. They had clearly gleaned some best practices from Teresa's guidance over that year, allocating substantial resources to support serious healing infrastructure.

The learning moment was that there were actually very few people who came into the church for this very organized and loving display of hospitality and healing. Of those who did come, very few were people of color. The church was majority white, so the demographics of the church volunteers made sense. Reflecting together later, Teresa and I discussed how the matching volunteer t-shirts, total absence of people of color in those shirts, and a summer camp check-in feel underneath outdoor tents before you could enter may have been more deterrent than invitation in the context of activists who may already have very valid deep distrust of the self-proclaimed inclusivity of church spaces. This was an amazing offering of care, and also a somewhat missed opportunity for the community who desperately needed what was, with great love and resources, provided.

So many learnings! In addition to forming TRACC, we developed an intentional distinction between *embodying* and *engaging* values and practices. In this context, embodiment comprises the layered healing practices *within* the individual and congregation, while engagement is how healing practices are offered *outside* the congregation. We share this model here for individual and congregational learning, framed in well relationships and well practices. By wellness we refer to the journey of reaching for our most abundant selves, individually and relationally. This wellness presents along a continuum that rejects the binaries of healthy or unhealthy, whole or broken, or even well or unwell. Let's be much more imaginative, embracing what wellness can be experienced in this life, in these bodies, and in our manifold contexts.

CONGREGATIONAL EMBODIMENT OF HEALING WORK

Embodiment is our nature and awareness of self, our way of being present with all of our senses as we experience our bodies, spirit, and stimulus from our environment. Embodiment also includes the development and practice of our values. Embodying is being.

Embodiment Praxis

1. Well Relationships

   a. Assess and support the health of relationships in your congregation, both with self and with others. While organizing, be intentional in addressing relationships as the health of these relationships will impact and be impacted by your organizing. Listening circles can aid your assessment. Employ the same approach as you would with small groups, with skilled healing facilitation.

   b. Accountability relationships should not be optional. Internal accountability within the congregation should have established guidelines to follow; external to the congregation, there should be identified, named community accountability. Every person organizing should know who they are accountable to and see that relationship as foundational to your shared ethic.

   c. It is vital that there is an equitable process of learning from and being in relationship with those at margins already doing healing work or the organizing issue(s) your congregation supports. Please also refer to the ways this book addresses cultural appropriation. Without these steps, the faith community will replicate the dysfunction/harm already present within the faith community.

2. Well Practices

   a. Incorporate healing practices in already established shared spaces: Bible studies, worship services, ministry meetings. Social change work is hard. You may experience things that are traumatizing. Leave room to prioritize individual as well as collective care. This means caring for the congregation and those who make up the congregation. Sustaining you, sustains healing, which sustains the work.

   b. Learn about contemplative/restorative practices like centering prayer, Lectio Divina, time in nature, mindfulness/meditation, body motion, and breath work. Incorporate the cultural healing practices already available within your congregational cultural context.

   c. We reiterate that having layered wellness practices is vital. Put resources into a team/ministry that can lead these wellness practices. Be trained. Train each other. Grow in wellness together. Recognize when the wisdom is not in the room. You are not going to know everything, and books are not the only way to learn. Seek relationships from healers already equipped to support individuals and the full congregation with the emotional impact of your organizing work. *Compensate healers and clinicians, particularly those of color.*

   d. Live into an ethic of do-no-harm. This necessitates continuously recalibrating your actions to align with your values. How are you expressing your values through everything from ministry policies, to creating healthy spaces, to your organizing infrastructure? Assess your individual and congregational responses when harm occurs. This would include those accountability relationships discussed in well relationships. We strongly encourage training in transformative justice and/or inviting transformative justice practitioners into your congregation.[6]

CONGREGATIONAL ENGAGEMENT OF HEALING WORK

Engagement is the application of our nature and deeply held values. Engagement is also how we interact with our environment. Engaging is doing.

Engagement Praxis

1. Well Relationships

   a. Remember that movement is a complex space of relationships and identities. You may not be invited into some spaces based on those factors. Be able to step back where you are less useful. Plan with colleagues/partners for having others who can show up when your presence complicates a space rather than offers healing. Continue to center the healing, not whether you must be the medium of the healing.

   b. Identify your congregation's primary role in the movement community and how healing is a part of that role. Individuals should also identify their own roles. Are you a healer in movement space? An organizer? Both? When you enter into community movement spaces it is important to know your role; find your own ethics and boundaries around how you are going to navigate the role(s) you hold.

   c. Financially and relationally invest in healers and clinicians in your community, especially healers of color. They have always been there. They were already in motion before you began.

2. Well Practices

    a. Invitation is key. Make sure when you are going into a community movement space you have been invited. Understand you may need to become a meaningful part of the community before your healing offerings are welcome. The people must know you enough to enter your space or for you to enter theirs, and then consent to receive the healing you offer.

    b. Be flexible in the ways healing spaces are curated. As discussed, relationships are key to holding impactful healing space. Allow these relationships to determine that impact, assessing how the healing space meets the needs of healers and community. There will be times that assessment means the healers go to the people in need of healing support, rather than the people coming to the place/space designated by the congregation for healing.

    c. Avoid doing the healing work alone. Find ways to work with a team or at least a partner. If support is not able to be present, there should be planned and consistent ways to check in by phone or virtually. Prioritize your collective congregational care as well as those you are caring for. Remember to engage care in the same ways you embodied individual and collective care.

    d. Examine your attachment to your healing work being paramount to the community. Folks may acknowledge the need for healing, but that doesn't mean that you will be able to provide care the way you expect, are used to doing, or on your own timeline.

e. Center humility. Know there is so much you aren't going to know or understand; be willing to understand, train, and educate yourself as you go. Be willing to do the work that is needed the day you show up—even if those tasks don't fit your framework of healing.

Center compassion, empathy, and grace. Movement space can be religious-skeptical at best and often religious-resistant. Part of the improvisation of movement care is knowing both what skills and capacities you can bring into a space *and* what is welcome and invited in. Sometimes that might just be the ministry of presence or listening. Plan ahead for what you will be offering and what might not be welcome. Make sure to ask the community what they want and need; bring that. We aren't asking that you hide or pretend you are not a person of faith; we're inviting you to honor that there are aspects of our faith that have not been the most kind to many people. Lean in to being in community with a diverse range of life and faith traditions and experiences.

* * *

BREATH FLOW
Make this the most satisfying breath
you have taken all day.
We are breathing with you.

* * *

We are living into a time of increasing urgency. We don't foresee the need for healing diminishing any time soon, but likewise, and in a beautiful and heartening way, there are more and more heartbeats leaning into healing ourselves, healing our communities, and healing our systems.

BIBLE BLUEPRINT: Ephesians 3:14–21

Preaching and teaching and sharing theology that limits God's ability to provide care for God's creation is theological malpractice. These images we bear are beautifully and wonderfully made in complexities that benefit from care and support that incorporate our beings as spirit, physical, and mental. Healing is available. May we faithfully reach for the fullness of joy and abundant life we are promised.
—*Vahisha Hasan*

Notes

1. This framing of healing is for the purposes of this chapter and the viewpoint of these authors/practitioners, Teresa Mateus and Vahisha Hasan.

2. See https://berenicedimas.com/consultations-herbal-medicine/.

3. Formerly University Park Baptist Church, the name at the time I joined this church body in August 2002.

4. Resmaa Menakem, *My Grandmother's Hands: Racialized Trauma and the Pathways to Mending Our Hearts and Bodies* (London: Penguin UK, 2021).

5. See our work here: TRACC: Trauma Response and Crisis Care for Movements, https://www.tracc4movements.com/.

6. There are many great resources available on transformative justice. A good place to start is Mia Mingus, "Transformative Justice: A Brief Description," https://leavingevidence.wordpress.com/2019/01/09/transformative-justice-a-brief-description/ as well as "Transformative Justice," Transform Harm, https://transformharm.org/category/transformative-justice/.

9

. . .

FROM POTLUCK TO POLICY REFORM
Creating Intergenerational Spaces

. . .

SANDRA SUMMERS

*To create bread assumes a particular kind of culture
that no longer simply gathers its food but works imagina-
tively and scientifically to transform the gifts of the earth
to some shared purpose or end.*

—Norman Wirzba[1]

If there is one thing many churches do well, it's potlucks. I have vivid memories of potluck Sundays as a pastor's kid. What new-to-me food could I sample? What sweet would my parents say yes to at the potluck that they wouldn't say yes to at the grocery store? And the question on everyone's mind, at every potluck: will there be enough? As I've moved into adulthood, those same questions enter my mind for every potluck, with the added question of: "Will my dish be the favorite of the event?" My love for potlucks has not wavered—just ask my wedding attendees who each brought a dish to share for the reception!

When we think about the idea of intergenerational space within our churches and organizations, it reminds me of how potlucks were organized in my two-stoplight, white rural small town. How do we include the young people? Make sure someone brings mac n' cheese. How do we include the older people? Make sure someone brings something fiber rich. Growing up in both suburban and rural churches, I have seen this potluck pattern time and time again. A vision would be named for intergenerational worship, so we added a coloring sheet and a large print bulletin to the existing liturgy. A hope would be named for more families to attend, so we added a carpet and used toys to the back of the sanctuary. For many churches and organizations, we stop here and throw up our hands, convinced that intergenerational spaces don't really work.

In a potluck approach to intergenerational engagement, we keep adding dishes to the table, marvel at the diverse spread, and give ourselves a pat on the back for how each of us contributed to the whole. What we often end up with is a cluttered table where no one exactly finds a space to be included. We have been preparing individual dishes, expecting a collective experience. With an intergenerational-potluck approach in our organizations and churches, we can, and have, produced impressive one-time events, but these are rarely sustainable or movement building. For intergenerational spaces to work, we need to walk away from the potluck and towards the kitchen together. From planning the menu to washing the dishes, justice-oriented intergenerational work is more akin to a homemade brunch with friends, sharing and creating together.

In middle school, I lived in a rural town of less than 3,000 people. My two-stoplight town would meet stereotypes of the rural Midwest, from the pride around the high school sports teams, to the lack of diversity, to the simple routines of small-town living. There was a desire in the community to reimagine and revitalize the town from its rather sleepy existence, so the city organized a revitalization task force. My dad took the lead in a sub-group focused on youth and families in the community. Along with others, he recruited youth to be a part of the citywide initiative. I joined the group a few years into the project (mostly because I thought the older kids involved were the coolest and some of their cool factor would become mine by association).

Joining the youth committee was a pivotal moment in what would become my framework for intergenerational spaces. Youth led the meetings and engaged with the adults at the table as equals. Through the committed and shared work of this group, we secured state grants to develop a recreation park in our town. The committee engaged the community to assess the needs and desires for what this park would include. The committee was not a space where the youth were treated as less than, nor was that the case for the adults; rather, it was a group who co-created the expressed needs of the community. It was not a potluck; it was a meal planned and developed within intergenerational relationships.

Since my time on my small-town youth committee, I have served on many committees in various spaces, from higher education to community organizations to local congregations. Being a five-foot tall petite woman, I am often perceived to be the youngest in the room. For years, I experienced extreme frustration about how this reality played out, finding myself regularly speaking for ages not represented at the table. Knowing what an intergenerational space looks like at its best drives me to continue to create those spaces at every table.

As my own years advance, I find that my category of "young" is a growing age range, while "old" is a shrinking age range. I find myself having to pause to not repeat patterns that have frustrated me for years. A mentor taught me the phrase, "God, help me not become that which I despise." I do not want to become one of "those old people" who only complains about "those young people." Because I deeply believe and know the power of spaces truly living out intergenerational relationships towards a common goal. Today, I follow in my dad's footsteps and work alongside the Youth Council of the Memphis

Interfaith Coalition of Action and Hope (MICAH) in Tennessee. By continuing to push to have the youth at the decision-making table, our organization is reaching a type of intergenerational thriving that our city has never seen.

Moving from a potluck mentality to a thoughtful meal approach creates tension. The first layer of tension engages different cultural understandings and assumptions of age. Every community has different beliefs that both uplift and minimize the gifts of different ages. On Confirmation Sunday, we highlight the young age at which Elijah heard God's call, but quickly dismiss youth joining committees or other areas of leadership. We may affirm the possibilities present in old age, rejoicing with Abraham and Sarah at the birth of Isaac when we celebrate someone's retirement, but determine someone is "too old" for a particular ministry. Unfortunately, there is a tendency in churches to highlight milestones as they relate to age without engaging in deep reflection about the ability of the Holy Spirit to work in and through age markers.

The second layer of tension to acknowledge is generational theory. Take a moment, right now, and in the margins of this page write out all the phrases you hear, and, to dig deeper, phrases you say, about different generations: Gen Z, Millennial, Gen X, Baby Boomer, Greatest Generation, etc. Take a look at what you wrote. Do your descriptions of others match the vision of a beloved community, or has our language around generational identity become yet another tool of the oppressor to minimize and divide our experiences based on our birth year?

The cultural obsession with generational theory is a blockage to lifegiving movement building work across the age span. And what most folks in the United States might not realize is that our obsession with generational labels is a new and unique phenomenon in our country. In order for us to move forward crafting meals together, we need to

look back at the history of how the potluck model of generational cat-
egorization was spoon fed to us through precision marketing.

The Strauss-Howe generational theory is where we see this language around generations emerge in the late 1980s–1990s. The basic
idea of the theory is that a cyclical pattern ushers in a new cultural
era about every twenty-ish years and that these eras influence the characteristics of those born within a certain cycle.[2] Of important note is
that this theory, although widely referenced in our society, is not based
in scientific research. In addition, it was a theory developed from
exclusively white history. Generational theory has contributed to the
"potluck" style of organizing by preventing space for the intersections
of what may be true for a generation to mix with race, class, ability,
gender, sexuality, and other identities to reveal a deeper, more complex, more Divine truth.

The combination of messages we were raised with about age, plus
the messages we have been sold, create a complex starting point when
engaging in the work of creating intergenerational spaces within our
churches and communities. We begin with the goal of intergenerational space, which often turns to interpersonal tension; but when we
dig deeper, justice-oriented intergenerational spaces start with intrapersonal work. Below is a series of questions that you are invited to
reflect on prior to engaging in intergenerational work. Find a group
of people that you are already in relationship with to start unpacking
your own understanding of and relationship with age:

CHANGE MAKER REFLECTION QUESTIONS

1. What messages were we taught (implicitly and explicitly)
   about age?

2. How do we feel about the messages we were taught?

3. Do we agree with the messages we were taught?

4. What do we ourselves think about our current ages?

5. What do we think, feel, and believe about the age of those closest to us (family, friends, co-workers, community members, etc.)?

6. What assumptions do we have about those younger than us? Older than us?

7. How do our words and actions perpetuate these assumptions? Do our words and actions reflect the beloved community?

8. How many of our relationships are with people our own age? How many meaningful relationships do we have with people not our age?

9. Where can we go in our own community to build relationships with someone of a different age?

10. What are we willing to change about our own behavior to be in relationship with people of different ages?

Intrapersonal work of every flavor is tough stuff, but knowing who you are when you enter a space has the power to change that space. After you, and a small group, have engaged with these ten questions, find others whose ages were not represented in that space to answer the same questions with you. Listen and notice points of connection and ask questions about where your thoughts diverge.

After intentional reflection, it is easier to see the power and value in intergenerational organizing. When a group of youth get ignored by the mayor for a request to meet, the headline reads differently and moves others in ways that wouldn't be true if it were retirees. When retirees wait in line on behalf of working parents for school supplies, that display of power moves others. As intrapersonal awareness grows, so too will the awareness of the unique gifts present across the lifespan.

Now, you've done the internal work and it's time to create something tangible. Start with the spaces you are in and write down what ages are and are not present. Then assess why. Be aware of the space taken up by different age groups in conversation. Are folks with kids the ones being listened to when hiring a family pastor? Are retirees the ones being listened to when developing a weekday book group? Beyond the congregation, are kids being included in your fights to keep antiracism centered in school curriculums? Are elders included when organizing against cuts to food and transportation services are on the line? In the book of Luke, Jesus sends the disciples out two by two, the biblical buddy system. Jesus was acting like an organizer by ensuring that the disciples were not alone in the work, and the same principle should be enacted when it comes to age. At decision-making, tables two of every age group that your church is seeking to engage should be present from the beginning. When people are in spaces together, the space changes. We are less able to hide behind cultural mores or clickbait summaries of an age bracket when we share communal space in person.

For many tables, the shift to include all generations may not be difficult. For other tables, this step may take intentional and targeted relationship building. Lean on the power of the one-on-one (intentional conversations where your goal is to listen and learn what motivates and inspires another person) (see chapter 2). No matter what table you find yourself at, the next practical step is to make a meal together. Food is not just a helpful metaphor in intergenerational work, it is an ideal praxis.

Plan a time and space to cook together and invite everyone who you want to be included in your movement in that initial planning phase. There are ways to engage all ages and abilities in the process of cooking. Many churches and community organizations have kitchens that are often empty and available throughout the week. Individuals will learn about others while chopping carrots or mashing potatoes. The young adult living alone may find a unique connection with the widower as they both struggle to figure out how to cook for one. The toddler who can't quite hold the big knife may connect with the person with limited hand mobility. Sharing a human experience creates human relationships. Completing the shared task of creating a meal together leaves a group more able to envision actions outside the kitchen.

The seemingly simple act of cooking together with all ages engaged will be more illuminating than one might assume. By cooking together, we learn more about people. We learn the realities of living with dietary restrictions and financial constraints. We learn about cultural norms other than our own and about food we didn't even know existed. From these shared experiences and cultivated relationships movement building work can, will, and does happen. When a group across the age spectrum feels empowered to know their role in the kitchen, is valued for their contribution, and participates in the planning and plating of an experience—that is holy movement towards the beloved community.

Now what? When the dishes are dried and put away from the first meal, we must resist the natural temptation to call the work done. Just as we need to eat daily, the work of intergenerational organizing requires daily sustenance in order to bring about radical change. Many churches specifically struggle to weave together youth and adult action. The framework below can be used with all ages. As a community is developing intergenerational organizing, it is best to have "both/and" when it comes to gatherings; in other words, have some age-specific gatherings to build power unique to that age bracket as well as joint spaces where all ages are present.

From the initial conversations and meal, the next goal is to identify potential leaders. Often, church spaces lack leaders from youth and young adults. Therefore, leader identification must include adults who are already in relationship with youth as they will not only be able to identify potential youth leaders, but they will be seen as trusted individuals to engage in organizing with young people throughout your church or organization. In addition to adults, youth with a current passion, curiosity, and/or drive for social change must be identified, sought out, listened to, and developed. Set up one-on-one conversations with these individuals to uncover what issues, ideas, and concerns are being heard and spoken of by youth. The goal of these conversations is to get them to say yes to cocreating an organizing group in your church, which may or may not be connected to an adult group. Next, set up an initial meeting with this small group of individuals (three to five people is plenty to start!) akin to the building of other groups and ensure each meeting includes the following three components:

1. Relationship Development

2. Power Building

3. Play

Relationship building includes icebreakers, one-on-ones, and other activities that give space for participants to share their story with others in the room with the goal of connection among members of the group. Prior to the initial meeting, ask everyone attending to be prepared to present an idea about what the group can do to build relationships. This ask is a simple tool not only to engage everyone, but to increase buy-in for what may otherwise be deemed "cheesy." It is also an opportunity to observe the ways that each individual in the small group approaches leading.

Power building, sometimes called political education, is similar to learning. Everyone needs to learn about the basics of community organizing, local civics, and issues you're taking action on. The more individual voices who lead these power building times, the better. Teaching should engage all learning modalities to ensure it is an environment that cultivates communal curiosity rather than an "I speak and you listen" kind of space. In addition to learning the "nuts and bolts" of organizing and issues, each person must learn what work they are called to. Mutual interest is vital. If the goal is to make tangible actions, one needs to know what they have the passion to see through to completion.

Play is vital to sustainable justice building. The work of justice is hard and serious. But without play, we can easily become that which we despise. There are plenty of current resources that highlight the physical and psychological benefits to play. Play is a tool of both relationship building and power building, and it is also an act of resistance. Crumple up an agenda and have an indoor snowball fight. Tape silly string under chairs before a meeting. Play board games, find some improv games, or dust off that foosball table that's been in the youth room for at least one full generation. If you have no idea what play could look like in your context, you have an excellent opportunity to ask for help from someone who you know knows how to play. (Note: This may not be the youngest person you know—it might be that person who just always seems to have a whoopie cushion in their pocket.) While playing, it may feel like you are "not doing enough," but what you are doing is both implicitly and explicitly modeling that justice building is to be life giving.

The model outlined above is what has developed through the forming of the MICAH Youth Council. Since the founding of the organization, adults have recognized the need and value in ensuring youth voices are a part of the organization. I was tapped as a potential leader by our now executive director after I casually mentioned that I enjoy working with youth. Other leaders poured into me the knowledge and skills for community organizing so that I could apply those learnings to the youth-created space. From there, I sought to find other adults who would help develop our team. I will admit that it has been a slow process to recruit, develop, and maintain relationships. Prior to the coronavirus pandemic we met once a month in a central location of town. Once a month was not frequent enough for tangible actions to gain traction past the recruitment/excitement phase. It took patience and genuine curiosity to be in relationship with others for the intergenerational space to be developed.

Once about ten youth were curious about justice seeking, we held a weekend retreat full of relationship development, power building, and play. The youth identified their primary concerns in their community and set their goals for what Beloved Community meant for them. Another adult leader and I assumed the position of being bumpers on the bowling alley of their trial-and-error development. The youth are in charge of the ball and the pins they are aiming for, while the adults help coach and guide as needed. This means that energy ebbs and flows with the school calendar. This means that their recruitment efforts with their friends develops more leaders than any presentation I or other adults could lead. This means that the space they have created is beyond anything I could have led them to alone.

Now, the youth have developed their own structure of leadership and engagement similar to what they have observed works in the adult spaces. During the coronavirus pandemic, the youth acknowledged that once a month was not frequent enough for them to reach the goals they sought for themselves. They now meet weekly for one hour to plan the upcoming week or tasks and actions. They are in daily communication about their goals and actions, relying heavily on a web-based texting platform (GroupMe) that is not dependent on having a cell phone, as many in our group do not yet have their own phone. Two representatives from the Youth Council are present at all meetings of the larger MICAH body and organization, with one of the adult coaches present to again serve as that "bumper," ensuring the youth voice is noticed and heard. Because we have been working at this model for a few years, the culture of the organization has shifted to assume the involvement of and engagement with the youth when it comes to anything the organization as a whole is crafting, developing, or doing.

We have noticed in our intentional intergenerational organizing that the youth are models for the adults for what it means to come to meetings prepared to do the work. There is a shared space for youth to learn from those who are older, but even more, there is ample opportunity for those who are older to be reminded of the gifts of the young. When the youth speak in our organization, they are prepared, use their allotted time on an agenda accordingly, and are able to clearly name their objectives. They know what they are cooking up and are inspiring (sometimes agitating) a new recipe of engagement for all of those present in the work.

Wendell Berry writes, "You can eat food by yourself. A meal, according to my understanding anyhow, is a communal event, bringing together family members, neighbors, even strangers. At its most ordinary, it involves hospitality, giving, receiving and gratitude."[3] In the Christian tradition, we celebrate Communion, or the Lord's Supper, as a central sacrament of our faith. This sacrament of communion was a meal with an unlikely community combination. At its best, intergenerational organizing is a meal with the goal of cooking up lasting recipes for a transformed world rooted in justice and love.

We live in hungry times. From physical hunger to spiritual hunger, we are all in need of a being fed a good meal. Whether you have a justice committee in your congregation, or simply the idea of one, it's time to get cooking.

RECIPE FOR INTERGENERATIONAL ORGANIZING

1. Gather the unique ingredients of your community
2. Sprinkle in curiosity of who is missing
3. Knead generational tension
4. Add a dash of play to taste
5. Finish with a heaping spoonful of prayer
6. Combine all ages
7. Enjoy!

BIBLE BLUEPRINT: Matthew 18:3

Grasp the imagery of this verse! If you grew up in some type of Sunday School setting you might even be picturing an actual picture. Jesus, hanging out on a rock with docile children on his lap (and, of course, a very clean, and seemingly silent, lamb off to the side). What is glossed over in the glossy image is Jesus's subversion of systems of power in this passage. Children represented those on the margins of power. The adults around the pristine preaching rock were arguing about their own greatness. Jesus tells them they must change by using a child as an object lesson. Jesus was telling the adults to take up less space, humble themselves, and see the gifts present in those on the margins. What would it look like to turn the frame of that Sunday School picture to see the shocked faces of the adults called out on their behavior? —*Sandra Summers*

Notes

1. Norman Wirzba, *Food and Faith: A Theology of Eating* (New York: Cambridge University Press, 2011), 13.
2. William Strauss and Neil Howe, *Generations: The History of America's Future, 1584 to 2069* (New York: William Morrow and Co., 1991); William Strauss and Neil Howe, *The Fourth Turning: An American Prophecy* (New York: Broadway Books, 1997).
3. Wendell Berry, *On Farming and Food* (Berkeley: Counterpoint, 2009).

SECTION III

· · ·

Building Up
Putting It All Together

10

. . .

RESISTANCE, RESILIENCE AND RENEWAL
Cultural Organizing for Congregations

. . .

Tracy Howe

The function of art is to do more than tell it like it is—
it's to imagine what is possible.

—bell hooks

CULTURAL ORGANIZING IN THE CHURCH

The church I was formed in as a youth began as a church plant that met in a middle school for a good number of years before breaking ground on a building in Boulder County, Colorado. It took a lot of work and organizing to pull off a worship service week after week in the middle school. I remember the smell and feel of the cold hymnals that were pulled out of the trailer and put on the chairs in the auditorium. I remember the different pastel-colored paper that parts of the bulletin were printed on, and the way my mother liked to go through the bulletin and bookmark all the hymns and any other pages she would need from the book of worship before everything started. I remember the puppet that came out for the children's sermons and the pastor who would tell us stories about what Baxter the plush basset

· 154 ·

hound had been through that week. The staple songs we sang every week and the parts of worship that were always the same, like saying, "peace be with you," were my favorite, and especially running to the altar after the benediction and sharing the leftover fresh baked communion bread with the other children.

When it was warm enough, there was a park next door and plenty of space for potlucks and play afterwards. Outside of the Sunday worship services I remember crafting and making special ornaments for the Advent season, taking collections of money, food, and goods year-round for different organizations and families in need, and even parties to mark the different seasons. This was in addition to the ongoing "church stuff": baptisms, confirmations, weddings, funerals, and people in general supporting one another within the congregation. Ministry groups would come through and share with our small church. Some of these programs deeply impacted my life because groups sang songs that awakened parts of my Spirit and spoke about being connected to people all over the world. This small church did not have a youth group or youth pastor, but I remember church, in these formative years, being a place of food, of ritual, of singing, of feeling, of learning, and of community. The church was all that for me in part because they were doing so much cultural organizing and I was able to engage and grow in it.

Culture refers to shared patterns of seeing, thinking, and acting. It emerges from shared symbols, narratives, values, rituals, and practices. Local churches are full of culture and cultural practices. Obviously, weekly worship itself is a ritual, but within a worship service there are shared symbols, narratives, values, rituals, and practices embodied and proclaimed every week: singing together, sharing the peace, taking the offering, sharing in Holy Communion, and more. Churches might use candles, colors for different seasons, altars, carefully designed sanctuaries, artwork on the walls, baptismal fonts, outside prayer gardens or labyrinths, sometimes fresh baked bread and wine or juice for communion and more. Anyone who volunteers regularly knows things don't just happen. The Advent wreaths don't just set themselves up. It takes organizing so that the collective body can participate in the culture, the singing of the songs, etc., towards a collective lifegiving outcome. Yes, the greeter signup and making sure the bulletin is made each week are cultural organizing within the local church.

Outside of worship, our cultural organizing shines just as strong, with coffee and fellowship hours, educational programming often involving music and arts, and the star of them all—the potluck! Foundational to cultural organizing is making culture accessible to all. We are sharing beautiful pieces of our culture and/or creative expression, but culture is not made apart from the collective whole. In successful cultural organizing, everyone is contributing, and they feel valued for it. The potluck is a great example because we tangibly see that it was a collective effort—including those who contributed gratitude and hungry bellies and good conversation! The community experiences nourishment because the time and fellowship are rich.

THE GOOD NEWS AND SOME CHALLENGES

Cultural organizing makes accessible the symbols, traditions, rituals, narratives, practices, and expressions to the collective whole towards a lifegiving outcome. The good news, as you can see, is that churches are already places of cultural organizing! Take note of where your church is most fully present to lean into where you, as a church, are already succeeding at cultural organizing. Your church is most certainly culturally organizing towards building community and fellowship through post-service fellowship hours and potlucks. Your church utilizes cultural organizing in planning for worship: preparing the space; hanging art, seasonal decorations, and liturgical banners; and preparing the materials necessary for the community to participate by printing bulletins or preparing projected slides or other multimedia. Perhaps your church has made a banner and participated in a community parade, or your choir has sung as part of an interfaith vigil. This too is cultural organizing. Maybe you are new to this vocabulary and framework, but you are not new to cultural organizing. The challenge now is to apply what you are already doing in your local church towards ongoing movement work and coalition organizing.

Before moving into coalition organizing (organizing with other groups), we must know where we are coming from. Javiera Benavente and Rebecca Lena Richardson, cultural organizers with Arts and Democracy, note that cultural organizing is about "organizing from a particular tradition, cultural identity, community of place, or worldview."[1] In cultural organizing as a faith community, we have shared narratives, traditions, and rituals that are informing our practices. However, I don't know a single church that is not working through something around history, tradition, doctrine, theology, or practice. These things are not settled and not neutral, and cultural organizing includes continuing the dialogues your church is no doubt engaged in, whether it is around what pronouns to use for God in the hymns, or what representation and images are used in the PowerPoint during worship. All of it is important and part of your ongoing journey.

The single best practice to incorporate in order to avoid the pitfall of racist and harmful cultural appropriation on your cultural organizing journey is to situate cultural expressions and practices in their historical context and in relationship to the church. It might seem redundant, like you are just reading the small print around the hymns in the hymnals, but this is literally what I am suggesting you do if you sing a hymn. Who wrote it? When was it written? What culture/language group/country does it come from? Then begin to say, "we sing this hymn in this community because _____."

This practice of naming our relationship and history to practice and place and community can extend to many things and should include who/what/why/where. Who are we as a church? Are we multiracial? Are we primarily Dutch? We are a community of specific people brought together because _____. That is our "who" and "why." Even if we hope that God is growing us into something beyond what we are now, it is important to name our roots and present reality in welcoming people. "Where" should include a Native land acknowledgement unless we are a church of Native people on our ancestral land. Maybe it also includes our watershed. And the "what" is anything we are using in worship or programming: a hymn, a quote, or a piece of art, for example. Naming things and locating ourselves and our connections to our practices, whether with hymns or other elements of church life, builds collective cultural memory, something white supremacy destroys, no matter what race the state declares us to be.

BEYOND THE BUILDING: CULTURAL ORGANIZING IN COALITION

Cultural organizing in coalition to change oppressive conditions is perhaps some of the most powerful and transformative work I have ever been a part of. The Highlander Center in Appalachia has engaged, led, followed, and trained organizers in cultural organizing in the South for generations. They say that "[cultural organizing] is always led by and accountable to the culture of the participants . . . Cultural organizing celebrates and honors people's spiritual traditions and cultural expression in the work to shift policies and practices."[2] This is a powerful definition for cultural organizing in movement space. My own definition for cultural organizing in faith communities echoes theirs: "towards a life-giving outcome" includes shifting unjust policies and practices. The depth, breadth, and impact of that outcome will have to do with strategy, not only tools, which we've already established local churches possess in abundance!

Let's take the practice of Holy Communion as an example and reflect on it in the framework of cultural organizing. By practicing it (organizing the practice of it) in different ways in and with community coalitions, we can make it accessible to the collective whole towards different lifegiving outcomes. Here are three different ways to leverage this cultural organizing; some of them involve moving into coalition building and movement work.

1. Holy Communion as part of a weekly worship service. I was formed in a church that had communion every week. We came together in a circle. The bread was torn from a common loaf, and we could drink from a common cup or take an individually poured glass. It took time. In this context, the cultural organizing is being leveraged towards spiritual renewal, resilience, and ongoing community building. These grounding practices are crucial and invaluable to our sense of belonging and being able to show up with and in our community faithfully for the long haul.

2. Holy Communion at the US/Mexico border, shared across the border wall. Increasingly, the border "wall" between the United States and Mexico is made of giant metal bollards. They do not allow the passage of a person, but bread and juice have been known to make it through by extending a hand between the bollards, or even throwing the elements over the top, according to some of the faith communities in the area. In this context, the cultural organizing has become a nonviolent direct action because it is taking place in a militarized zone in direct defiance of what the state is attempting to do: separate and isolate people. Depending on how this action is shared with the general public, the cultural organizing can be leveraged towards a specific policy effort, or general advocacy for immigration reform. It can also be leveraged to build joy and solidarity

among communities being directly impacted by state violence. Regardless, once we are working towards an outcome on behalf of a community directly impacted by injustice (we are all impacted by injustice but not all directly impacted)—in this case people impacted by the militarized border and border policies—our work must be in coalition with these people and center these leaders and voices in any kind of organizing.[3]

3. Holy Communion using bread made by migrants stuck at the border. Since the forty-fifth presidential administration instituted a policy called the "Migrant Protection Protocols," which require anyone seeking asylum to remain in Mexico for the duration of their asylum-seeking process, and other policies such as Title 42, an exceedingly harmful CDC policy invoked to prevent people from even seeking asylum in the first place during the COVID-19 pandemic, there has been a swelling of people stuck living on the Mexican side of the border. Extremely vulnerable, they have relied on one another and those willing to help them to survive, some for years, on the Mexico side of the border wall instead of with communities and family members in the United States.

In Southern Arizona at this time, many churches realized they needed to move their asylum support efforts south of the border. One project that emerged as an ecumenical effort is Casa de la Misericordia in Nogales, Sonora, which offers shelter and hospitality to families who, in different times, might be able to seek asylum and argue their cases in the United States. As a way to build solidarity with the migrants living at "La Casa," church leaders planned to share fresh baked bread in solidarity for World Communion Sunday. A delegation of pastors from southern Arizona visited La Casa de la Misericordia (the House of Mercy) where a traditional bread oven exists, and together with the migrants, they made bread. Some was then brought back across the border and shared with churches as part of communion during Sunday worship. This cultural organizing was leveraged towards solidarity, education, joy, resilience, and community building. It was communion shared across the border but did not escalate tension with the state, which is what nonviolent direct action does (with strategic and powerful purpose). It built on culture, ritual, and tradition already present (World Communion Sunday) and organized around that.[4]

These are just three examples, based on actual occurrences. There are many more to be certain. I've been to churches where communion was celebrated as a house party and that house party could certainly go public! Cities across the United States are effectively criminalizing the experience of homelessness by passing ordinances aimed at this vulnerable population that make it illegal to pass out food in public parks or lay down on benches. What would serving open communion in a park with and among our siblings experiencing homelessness do? What about moving beyond communion and seeing your church's ability to throw a good potluck as a cultural organizing tool? Where, when, and how could this be leveraged towards a lifegiving outcome? How can you move beyond acting as a single congregation into coalition organizing with this tool?

As your imagination expands, stay rooted in the other practices you are learning throughout this book. Understanding what leaders and voices to center and how to stay grounded in and accountable to the greater community is key to both being successful and being liberated along the way! We are free to not figure out and do everything all at once, or ever! Through deeper and more effective cultural and community organizing, we are capable of becoming more authentic communities, learning how to be more present and public with ourselves and our resources, and how to show up more faithfully in the work and journey of justice making. This work is not about doing more and certainly not about knowing more than others; it is about living deeper and being more connected and more present in our communities. It is about being more spiritually alive. By "spiritual," I do not mean disembodied—quite the opposite! Spirituality can be defined as the demonstration of living relationships. The depth of our spirituality, then, is the depth to which we can demonstrate living relationships with self and creation, neighbors known and unknown, generations past and future, and God/Creator/Spirit/Justice/Beauty/Jesus . . .

CULTURAL ORGANIZING IN MOVEMENT WORK

Just as I was able to access ritual and the traditions of my faith because of the cultural organizing in my local church during my formative years, I have been able to participate and persevere in ongoing movement work because of the cultural organizing. First of all, it's often cultural organizing that allows for the effective sharing of narrative through images, stories, documentaries, songs, social media, and zines about what is actually happening. As I am writing, there is a mainstream media blackout on all the resistance action around stopping the Line 3 pipeline through Minnesota and Anishinaabe Territory. However, because of the incredible cultural organizing happening there, including filmmaking, storytelling, social media and more, hundreds of people from all over the country continue to arrive at different Water Protector camps to support the efforts to shut down the catastrophic and violent project started by Enbridge. During the Ferguson Uprising, there was a similar mainstream media blackout, and organizers Johnette Elzie and DeRay McKesson coedited a daily Ferguson protest newsletter. In Charlottesville, when multiple groups of armed white supremacists descended onto the city the summer of 2017, we knew we would need photographers and visual storytellers who would be able to capture the defiance of the antiracist activists refusing to let white supremacy and fascism take over that day or any day; we raised funds and brought in photographers who were trained and experienced in that setting.

I have encountered many people living in the tension of being actively engaged in their community of faith, which informs and grounds their concern for and commitment to justice in the world, and concern for "activists" engaged in the streets in protests and direct action, but not knowing how to get from weekly worship services to rapid response community organizing in which they might show up publicly with their greater community. Maybe this is you! You clearly see and feel the call to action and presence in the streets and are trying to figure out how to show up in solidarity in the community. Cultural organizing is at least one tool in your organizing belt you already have and can show up with for the cause of community building and justice. Cultural organizing can be mobilized "in the street," but it is also necessary within and through the entire movement ecosystem. Who is feeding all those protesters before and after the action? What about during the meetings? What about their children? Get that potluck tool out of your cultural organizing tool belt and show up with and for your community. What you serve and the way you serve will and should speak to the culture of your community and congregation.

THE WORK OF THE PEOPLE

I am a cultural worker and a liturgist. "Liturgy" means "the work of the people," and faith communities use it to order their rituals and prayers to create "liturgies." In my opinion, any liturgy should be specific enough to locate us historically, geographically, and culturally, as well as theologically, even though there are universal struggles and symbols that will rise and threads that carry over from one place to another and from one generation to another. Writing liturgy has been invaluable in documenting the movement, in gathering people— whether they were religious or not—and in sharing and raising spiritual and practical awareness of the moment.

In Charlottesville, on August 11, 2017—before the assaults began and neo-Nazis threw fire and fists and other weapons at students and community members gathered around the statue of Thomas Jefferson in front of the Rotunda at the University of Virginia, before the worst of the violence broke out—there was invitation, invocation, and mass cultural organizing in the form of an interfaith prayer service. People had flown in from around the country answering a national call to stand against white supremacy and participate in nonviolent direct action alongside community members in Charlottesville who had been organizing and training for months, knowing what was about to descend on the city the next day for the unite the right rally, the largest white supremacist gathering in US history. The night before, we had three tasks as organizers: 1) to impart our context and moment in Charlottesville; 2) to demonstrate our shared stakes; and 3) to extend an invitation to action. There were community members of all faiths and none, and some skeptical (at best) of what we faith leaders were organizing in the first place. We had a flash point to impart something of the larger story and the reason for us coming together, as well as a small window to offer something to connect and anchor all the different collective work of the next day. The verse chosen for its shared place in Muslim, Jewish, and Christian scriptures was Psalm 118:19–20: "Open up the gates of justice that I may go through and give thanks to God. This is God's gate; the just shall go through." I wrote an emancipatory psalm based on the text, read by three different faith leaders gathered that evening.

PSALM 118, EMANCIPATORY READING BY REV. TRACY HOWE

[5]Out of my distress I called out;

Out of the distress in Charlottesville we called on communities
of faith.

God answered and set me in a broad place.

I took a deep breath and took in the vastness of God's space.

[6]Grounded in God's love, I do not fear.

What can mortals do to me? What can racism and hate do to me?

What can the alt-right do to me? What can the

militarized police do to me?

[7]God's love is with me; when I act in that love;

I shall look in triumph on those who hate me.

[8]It is better to take refuge in God

than to put confidence in guns or security built by men.

[9]It is better to take refuge in God

than to put confidence in the presidents or the CEOs.

[10]Patriarchy surrounded me;

in the name of the Lord I smashed it!

[11]Racism surrounded me, white supremacy surrounded me on
every side;

in the name of the Lord I cut it down!

[12]Hate and violence surrounded me like bees;

they blazed like a fire of thorns;

in the name of the Lord I cut them off!

[13]I was pushed hard, so that I was falling,

but the Lord helped me.

[14]She is my strength and my might;

God has become my salvation.

[15]There are glad songs of joy in the tents of the justice doers:

[17]I shall not die, but I shall live,

and recount the deeds of the Lord.

[19]Open to me the gates of justice, *abran las puertas de la justicia*
that I may enter through them
and give thanks to the Creator.
[20]This is the gate of the Lord;
the righteous shall enter through it, those who do justice in love.

As the psalm was read, it became like a live poetry event. People cheered and responded after different lines. It did not seem to matter if one was familiar with the text or not. This was a reading for that moment. We were being prayed into togetherness. Reading and responding to the psalm was building a collective memory. There was hopeful anticipation grafting onto our cells as we read ancient words and prayed a new vision of justice.

CULTURAL PRACTICE

Here are three practices you can do as a congregation to deepen your cultural organizing.

1. *Audit your worship and liturgy materials.* If someone read just the prayers, hymns, and sermons, would the person know anything about your community's cultural location? Justice commitments? History? What do you learn by taking the time to locate each hymn and song you sing culturally and by year, and by naming your community's connection to the music?

2. *Identify the Native peoples whose land your congregation meets on.* Acknowledge the land and unless you are a Native faith community, create a ritual to hold the questions, discomfort, and anything else that surfaces with the acknowledgement that you are a community of settlers. When people ask about your church, consider answering by naming the ancestral land your community meets on.

3. *Hold an Imagination Lab.* Where/when would having an open table potluck in your community become an act of resistance? Resilience? Renewal?

Cultural organizing can help us understand our shared humanity and deepest interconnections, to hear the songs of the ancestors or of the generations not yet born, the weeping from distant times and the joy and beauty of what is possible. Cultural organizing grounds the community in practice, and through the act of singing, or dancing, or listening, or breaking bread together, we can pause and come back into our bodies and reconnect to the reasons we show up, both individually and collectively. Cultural organizing is collective power because as we gather, we also summon the wisdom and the beauty of our people past and present through ritual and art. To leverage this collective power for justice is a critical strategy that faith communities are well equipped for. Integrating it as daily practice will sustain us in the movement.

BIBLE BLUEPRINT: Mark 7:1–4

The people of the Bible lived in a rich and varied context of culture. Their music, clothes, food, language, and familial and communal ways are laid out in the text just as are their individual and collective struggles and victories. The ways in which they made it to and through comes forth in their stories, how they lived together, and the rituals they honored and adapted across generations. We should deepen our understanding of the cultural contexts in the text just as we should deepen and honor our own, in our lives and our stories still being written. —*Vahisha Hasan*

Notes

1. Javiera Benavente and Rebecca Lena Richardson, "Cultural Organizing: Experiences at the Intersection of Art and Activism," Animating Democracy, http://

animatingdemocracy.org/resource/cultural-organizaing-experiences-intersection-art-and-activism.

2. "Cultural Organizing," Highlander Research and Education Center, https://highlandercenter.org/cultural-organizing/.

3. Frontera de Cristo, a border ministry of the Presbyterian Church (USA) in Douglas, Arizona, and Agua Prieta, Mexico regularly celebrate "Agape Feasts" in which communion is shared on both sides of the border wall and elements are passed through the bollards. The first series of Agape Feasts began in 2005 to demonstrate a counternarrative to the minutemen who had begun deploying in that area. The minutemen were a white supremacist, anti-migrant armed militia terrorizing the region and searching for migrants crossing the desert. See Frontera de Cristo's website: http://fronteradecristo.org. Border Church is a church that formed specifically for the purpose of sharing communion together in spite of the militarized border at its western most point where it extends into the Pacific Ocean around Tijuana and the greater San Diego area. Congregants met at Friendship Park on both sides of the border weekly, but eventually the border was further militarized, preventing even this. Still people gather on both sides and resist. See the Border Church website at: https://www.borderchurch.org.

4. The delegation was organized in 2021 by Comunidad Limen in Tucson and Good Shepherd UCC in Sahuarita, Arizona. La Casa de la Misericordia is an ecumenical ministry of the Episcopal Diocese of Arizona, the Grand Canyon Synod of the ELCA, la Diocesis de Occ. de MX. and the S.W. Conf. of the UCC. See The Episcopal Diocese of Arizona, http://fronteras.azdiocese.org/.

11

. . .

RURAL ORGANIZING FOR
RURAL CONGREGATIONS

. . .

CHRIS DAVIES

When asked to contribute this chapter, I didn't feel qualified to write about rural organizing. What do I know about organizing? I grew up in a town of 5,000 people where at one point, as rumor has it, there were more cows than people, and the stoplight down by Route 44 with the Mobil gas station was *the* destination on a chilly autumn night. To go anywhere, you had to hop in the car and drive for a bit to see where the streets start to shine in fluorescent light and the houses get closer together. I grew up going to church as a given, even though not everyone did, and the ones who didn't were a bit out of the norm; but at that point, I don't remember noticing the stigma that those who experienced it would likely now call formative within their own early un-belonging.

I walked to high school, where I was in a class of about sixty kids, and whiteness was the unacknowledged standard. I remember, now, the differences that were singled out in race and class and religion. I remember, now, the teacher who tried so hard to activate us, teaching texts of liberation and watching *Schindler's List*, having a frank conversation about whether you read aloud the n-word in *To Kill a Mockingbird*, while studying the lyrics of songs we heard on the radio with absolutely no context of culture to compare it to. I remember the history teacher with a white-supremacy washed Americanized history who brought the Bible into the classroom and described his commitment to the conservative politics of the day, each day, and how history could be lifted and plucked to support the values he lifted.

Values came to me in different contexts: through each of the teachers and the education that we received in the classrooms; through the dance school and Irish culture classes my mom taught all through my childhood, and the Irish-adjacent ethnic communities that came with them. Values came through the congregation that gave an endcap to each week in youth groups, and through sermons with relatable metaphors and a stretch towards what could be, by the Grace of God and the actions of our own.

I remember learning about social movements and activists in pieces all around: through the news and media stories, and through their remembering the Civil Rights Movement in February each year. I remember listening to my own family talk about the movements they had some participation in, like my paternal grandmother marching for abortion access or the ways my maternal Irish family was loosely connected to the political troubles and poverty going on back home in Ireland, and then how they moved here to the States. Later, I remember hearing about my uncle who grew up here the next generation out, but then left the country swearing never to return so long as communists were stigmatized and sensationalized. I remember forming opinions about these things in ways that had me idolizing the activists and the people brave enough to speak for what they believed in, in front of so many people. And all this movement awareness amplified when I came out at sixteen—listening to how the teachers and leaders spoke of people with whom I related, and the conversations that brought queer folks to the forefront.

I soaked in everything I could learn, quickly, applied the learnings and understandings to a call to "make this world a better place," which is most of the language I had for all this at the time. Being the only out queer taught me a version of allyship and a way of approaching others with grace and curiosity about difference, rather than fear. At that point, I focused on action—leaping before I figured out what was happening and just trying to make it better. I didn't think it was organizing. I understood my role as living into my faith and a collective call to make this world a better place, oriented towards justice and loving all people with compassion and grace.

* * *

At the invitation to write, I still didn't think of my early experience as organizing. The people that I know who organize are so savvy in language and care, so connected to each other and the work, and they seem so *cool* with speaking gigs and books and boldness. They were at ease with songs from liberation movements past and had easy access to language to identify what's happening in systems around them. The people I know who organize *are* still all that! And I realized that what I grew up doing was organizing, too.

It's so different, and so interconnected. Even the language of the organizing stories was a barrier to seeing myself in it for a long time. The imposter syndrome of "why me? I'm just doing what I need to!" held me back from forming wider relationships.

And yet, it's the relationships between folks that makes organizing *function*. People show up when it matters to the people who are important to them. Today, any committed organizer, in any context, will say that the first rule of organizing is to *know* the people, get close to where it hurts, and work together to make it better.

However, because rural organizing felt so different than the stories I had access to, I didn't know how to connect them.

Rural organizing is a quiet slumber of relationships built over decades of showing up for people in projects and challenge and joy.

Rural organizing is a giant, scarred with pockets of poverty and pain, and inextricably connected to the land through the economies that employ the majority of households.

Rural organizing is knowing who has what shift at the family bar on the corner and which night was the potluck at the church every month where there's free babysitting.

Rural organizing is when your kid's best friends' parents are the neighbors no one particularly likes, and you have to take a deep breath and bring a thank-you side dish and snack over for the sleep-over—and yet when it comes down to it, those neighbors are the most trustworthy with your own kid.

Rural organizing is all about relationships between people who are radically different and inextricably connected—in ways that some could call mutual aid.

And I think that the barrier between rural organizing and the work of the movement organizations that prioritize ballot issues and revolutionary causes is often the language that we use to speak about it, not the actions which we are all demonstrating.

For example, to be a pastor is to be a type of organizer. All the same skills of leading volunteer groups and committing to work together on a project because we can believe together in a world that is better for all the people in it, rather than the one we see in evidence before us—that's organizing.

If you're a rural pastor or lay leader, you're an organizer already, and more savvy about the internal relational dynamics within your town than most. Through prayer lists and town gossip, rural pastors and church leaders usually know the families, what they're experiencing, and what's important to them. They know the places where the community aches, sometimes through the people coming in and asking directly for help, and sometimes through seeing the patterns that repeat themselves, again and again. If your experience in a small town is like mine, and you've picked up this book to learn how to connect into the things worth organizing for, then I hope that you are assured in knowing that the same skills that you use in gathering your community together for the causes your church holds dear—whatever they are—are the skills necessary to draw on in participating in the collective liberation of your community and beyond.

Church is one of those places where transformation is possible, and yet, in my experience, it is a slow and grace-filled process. One does not grow into oneself overnight—it's a loving journey of encouragement and care—and a journey that rural churches can know so well with their community that they do it without thinking—like breathing.

It's something like the monthly potluck. There's a group of people who bring it all together (organize it) with the hope that something will happen during the time (strengthen the relationships). They—often the affectionately called "church ladies," or the Grand Mistresses of the Meal—will gather the people and assign who makes what and ask the pastor to pray at a certain time. Perhaps church committees casually set up their tables and presentations, and there's a speech or two for what's coming. There is a shared purpose of gathering, which requires the intensive labor of a select few, and oftentimes there are hidden resentments of who does what and how often in the background. This, my colleague Rev. Elizabeth Dilley would say, is people being people-y. I find such wisdom in that assessment, because in any group of people there will always be some tension as people figure out how to be in relationship with one another.

The ideals of Christianity point to a way of relationship: Love your neighbor. Clothe the naked. Welcome the stranger. Free the prisoner.

Share the wealth. Set the table. Feed the hungry—and many congregations have programs that directly align with these calls on the interpersonal level and address the immediate pain and need. Organizing is what happens when we lift our eyes to the hills and see the ways in which society around us allows unrelenting oppression to happen with more and more vicious clarity towards those who are the most and multiply oppressed.

Organizing is what happens when we wonder aloud why the school system doesn't have enough money for books for the children and is the primary supplier of food for many families, and then the pastor and key church members are at the town council meeting saying how important faith is in our vote towards equity and making certain that all children have access to resources and food. Organizing is what happens when we start to point the gathering forces of Christian relationship towards the aches and pains in the collective whole.

After all, people are surprising. I know many a pastor who carries a story about a cranky critic who found connection only through their public complaints about the sermon, to the chagrin of the entire community—and then bequeathed their wealth to the collective through the church upon passing. Or the volunteer committee chair who has a moment of clarity about how their obnoxious leadership style has driven away any help, when the project at hand has died—and thus a humble revelation of learning follows. Or the guest who graced the church with their presence, once, and heard explicit welcome for themself in all their gender expressive glory, following the opening words: "No matter who you are or where you are on life's journey, *you are welcome here . . .*" and broke down with transformation and an outpouring of spirit to go on another day, another week, another year.

Pastoring is organizing. Church lay leaders are organizers. Ministry is an organized effort. And the worthiness of the work that happens in your context towards the collective good is translatable, when lifting attention from the symptoms to the sources. There's a particular kind of rugged stubbornness connected with faith. We carry on in limping institutions because we believe there is something worth gathering for. We have forty collective hours' worth of meeting conversations for a two-hour event. We gather digitally, or in dingy basements, or in the frozen aisle of the supermarket in the town over because it *matters* when we pause to have a conversation and say, "how are you," and "what's new in your world?"—even and especially when it feels awkward upon leaving and no one really got it right, but we all still tried.

The faith that the work we do together matters, no matter how asinine, is the faith that makes movements happen. In conversation with a dear friend and ACLU organizer, Melekte Melaku, I heard her speak about how critical the rural areas coming into the conversation were when she was working on Ohio Issue 1 in 2018. This ballot initiative for a state constitutional amendment would have begun to unravel the insidious sentencing and disproportionate impacts of the War on Drugs by releasing people from state prisons for low-level, nonviolent crimes. The cross-regional organizing—urban to rural—was critical, and from what I have understood, one of the places where the lack of clear relationships as well as the power dynamics hurt the hoped-for outcome of the vote on the constitutional amendment. Messaging didn't reflect the real diversity of the constituents.

According to Melekte, the conversations happening in various contexts were so radically different. The content presented was polarizing, and while that sometimes can be activating in urban/suburban areas, it had an adverse impact in rural communities. Because the currency of change is relationship, people seek to connect the issue to the folks they know, and the difference of experience between a town like the one I grew up in (or so much smaller!) with little or benign police interaction and predominantly urban areas where there is concentrated police violence against Black and Brown people points to a disconnect in messaging that can be mitigated by relationship and by understanding. The kind of violence from the systems of oppression that impact rural communities are different than what was messaged, and yet, connected. When the stories are (finally!) heard through relationship, especially around shared oppression, then solidarity becomes more easily forged through those relationships, resulting in cross-class, multiracial coalitions. When folks connect in relationship across difference, the stories of neighbors near and far become important! People show up when it matters to the people who are important to them.

And that's where I think we, folks coming from rural areas and leading in small towns, need to get out of our own way. We have to show up! In some ways, I still feel like a small-town girl: a bit awed by the world around me and naive to the way people in groups can be with each other, and ever optimistic towards something transforming, and willing to work for it. When a neighbor asks for help, you *help* them. That also means that I have to take the risks of getting it so very wrong, all the time, and of stumbling through conversations where I don't have the right words, trusting in the rugged faith and the collective outcomes that prioritize a Christian call towards equity and justice. I have to be brave enough to cold-call someone organizing near me and say, "hey, I'm not exactly sure what you're doing—but I believe in it and I believe it will help us all do better with one another," approaching with humility and asking where my energy fits into the whole.

With an even wider lens, it means we have to *find* the people who are organizing near our communities, or the organizations that hope to. That part, beloveds, is easier than it seems: look to the places where your people hurt. Listen for the divine push that whispers, "it didn't have to be this way," and "what would a world without this pain look like?" and "what's my role in bringing about the kin-dom of God, today?" When you've listened to the people, you can not only accompany them on their paths, but also learn about what sources of pain are present. I cannot stress enough that the research and relationship of *who is already doing this, and how do I connect with them?* is the first step. Do not fall into the trap of thinking only your church is working on it. We must lift our attention and our eyes to the systems and circumstances from which oppression comes, and recognize how we need each other, inside and outside the church, to catch a glimpse of the whole and help shift it. Organizing in rural communities is deeply connected to the issue areas that are literally already on our doorsteps.

Call the town office front desk folks, the superintendent of schools, the nearby hospital ER workers. Ask where the people hurt, and where the gaps are. And go into those conversations assuming that you, as the leaders and members of the local church, are also people worth knowing, in the shared work of showing up in your community. The problems that keep your community up at night, as Rev. Traci Blackmon says, could be overdose prevention and support, or the economic impact of jobs leaving town, or perhaps the lack of public housing, or needing collective support with healthcare when folks get sick and the hospital is far. Or like in my experience, perhaps it was more social action. As the only queer person I knew, I organized what was then called a Gay Straight Alliance—and learned of so many more people like me, including the gay elders right in my community who continue to lead and guide me, grounded by their history. Starting there was the beginning of the journey of gathering with people to make something happen to "make the world a better place."

And then, you will likely find that once you're working on something in your own community, you'll see the webs of connection between it all. You'll find the language of intersectionality as first coined by Kimberlé Crenshaw, and the people committed to liberation in their communities, and relationships that call you into working alongside them, and them into working alongside you. We need each other.

As people of faith and leaders in faith communities, we already have the *why*. We speak our call into action every Sunday in service and call each other into accountability towards Christian witness and action aligned with justice and God's call for us in the world. We already have the reserves of ritual and connection that will sustain us in the terrible failures and carry the momentum past the grand successes. We have an understanding that the work is neverending and have generations behind us to lean on in catching our breath, and a leadership development strategy to raise up the radicals of the future. We have the structure of success already before us. It's the shift towards aligning that effort from symptom to source that makes our work of pastoring, of leading church communities, move towards organizing.

BIBLE BLUEPRINT: Matthew 22:34–40

You can find this teaching throughout the Bible in a variety of phrasings and contexts. Paul says "Love is the fulfilling of Torah" (Romans 13:10), which is to say, the fulfilling of everything, which is to say, love is everything. And love, which we might call action to fulfill creation's well-being, is the ground from which organizing grows. We organize because we love our people, the land, the plants, the animals. We organize because we love the wind and rain and moon and stars. We organize because we love God. We organize because we love. We love, and so we organize. —*Anne Dunlap*

12

. . .

COMMUNITY SAFETY
An Incarnational Practice of Vulnerability

. . .

Nichola Torbett and Logan Rimel

Now faith, hope, and vulnerability abide, but the greatest of these is vulnerability.

—Rev. Lynice Pinkard, "Embracing Love's Ugly Baby"[1]

The Black members of our congregation had questions for us white members: "What does it mean to you to proclaim that Black Lives Matter? Do they? Do we? And what are you willing to do if that's the case?"

Late on a Sunday afternoon in 2016, the members of the First Congregational Church of Oakland (FCCO) were in our monthly meeting. I admit that I had thought this agenda item would be a slam dunk, that of course everyone would agree that we should hang a Black Lives Matter banner on the front of our highly visible building. We were a small, multiracial, social justice–oriented congregation, and many of us were activists well known in movement spaces and at city hall. "Black Lives Matter" was being preached nearly every Sunday from our pulpit. We were sincere; we all knew that.

But the Black members had questions. They wanted to know if we white members were willing to do more than say the words, if we were willing to do more than *appear* to support the movement because it looked good, or to ask *other people* to change policies that didn't necessarily affect us. Were we willing to change our own ways of doing things? Were we willing to become vulnerable ourselves?

In short, they were asking us how we together were going to *incarnate* our espoused values? How were we going to make them real and alive in the world?

What ensued was a long conversation about our church's relationship to policing. As a busy urban community center—home to five nonprofit tenants and four congregations as well as many community meetings—our small staff, members, and friends sometimes called the police. The church is known in the community as a place where people can come if they need help—with grocery gift cards, diapers, transportation vouchers—and sometimes people needed more help than we knew how to give; on occasion, when things escalated and someone got scared, that person would call the police. Police were also called onto campus to address vandalism and assist with health crises.

We knew the reality of policing in America: police harassment of Black people used to fund city governments; the peaceful protest at Standing Rock met with fire hoses in the North Dakota winter; "stop-and-frisk" policing traumatizing a generation of young Black and Brown men; Black and Brown men imprisoned disproportionately to create ill-paying jobs for poor whites and simultaneously lining the pockets of corporations; white people weaponizing the police to punish Black people for simply existing in a space; the endless horror of Black and Brown people murdered by police and the deep cynicism that involved officers will ever be held to meaningful account. That afternoon, we had to confront the truth: *Every time we brought police onto our property, we put people's lives in danger,* especially the lives of Black and Brown people, people who appeared visibly poor, and people with disabilities. And that meant we weren't a safe community for everyone.

We began to discuss together questions like: "What actually makes us safe or unsafe? Are we willing to risk anyone else's safety in order to minimize our own risk? Whose safety are we willing to risk and under what circumstances?"

These questions can't be answered once and for all, but as soon as we started talking about them, we realized that we needed to reduce our reliance on policing. On Good Friday, 2018, we held a press conference and publicly committed to "reimagining our policies, procedures, and relationships to our neighbors to reduce our reliance on policing that is too often deadly for those already marginalized, to contribute to restorative/transformative approaches to addressing harm, and to increase our capacity to ensure the safety of everyone in our community."[2]

We recognized that avoiding calling the police is no simple commitment; it would require identifying what situations would ordinarily initiate police contact and building community skills toward first response. We needed to get trained.

IF WE CAN'T RELY ON POLICE, WHO CAN WE RELY ON?

Very quickly, we realized that we couldn't incarnate this proclamation alone. We needed our neighbors. That is how the Alternatives to Policing Coalition was born and how I (Logan) got involved.

At first, we reached out to organizations with whom we already had relationships—our tenant organizations, those connected to our local Interfaith for Black Lives affinity group, organizations who had space nearby. A few signed on. A few more organizations joined when Showing Up for Racial Justice's Faith Organizing Project started a campaign called "Community Safety for All,"[3] asking churches to make a commitment to divest from policing. We got a grant. Our member organizations each pitched in four-hundred dollars, or whatever they could afford, to create our first budget, which would cover a series of trainings for our member organizations and the public. (We paid trainers five-hundred dollars each for a three-hour training and had co-trainers wherever possible; that was the primary expense beyond a few dollars for snacks. Meeting space was donated by member organizations.)

But before we could begin offering training, we had to agree on some guiding principles and practices that would shape our work. That led us to develop our shared values and agreements.

WHO WILL WE BE TOGETHER? HOW WILL WE BE TRUSTWORTHY?

If you want to "protest policing," well, there are physical places with signs out front where "policing" can be found. But the institution of policing—the officers, weapons, badges, and cages—is merely an incarnation of cultural values of domination and control, fear and alienation, exploitation and disposability, all in a setting of white supremacy and settler colonialism.[4] The institution of policing as we now know it is what happens when these values take on flesh to answer the question, "What does safety mean and how is it created?"

Many of us no longer agree with the answers our culture has given for those questions. If we are to incarnate something different, we must begin with our values or else risk recreating the institution that causes so much suffering. Most of us have been so inundated with the values of policing that we find them taking on flesh in our own actions and within our most treasured communities. We act as police to ourselves and each other. It is deep, healing work to learn instead how to incarnate relationship, vulnerability, and trust, and this is the work that we take on when we attempt to answer the safety question for our own communities.

(Some) Values That Incarnate as Policing	(Some) Values that Incarnate as Community*
White supremacy	Antiracism
Settler colonialism	Centering those most harmed or at risk
Domination and control	
Fear of each other	Interdependence
Separation from neighbors	Integrity and authenticity
Exploitation of people for profit	Compassion
People are disposable and can be sent "away"	Humility and courage
	Healing
Binary thinking (guilty/ innocent)	Responsibility and accountability
Guilty people deserve punishment	
Once guilty, always guilty	Sharing and sustainability
Individualism	Transformation and growth
Private property matters more than life	Collective liberation and possibility
Toxic masculinity	Learning and practice

We are deeply grateful to the Bay Area Transformative Justice Collective whose list of values provided our starting point.

Once we had a clear set of shared values, we had to think about how we would incarnate those values in our work together. What were the concrete practices that would bring to life a real alternative to policing?

These are the shared practices we have agreed upon, with gratitude to *The Body Is Not an Apology*,[5] from which many of these were borrowed:

Bring our bodies, not just our minds, into the space

Embrace multiple perspectives and cultivate curiosity

Have compassion for and honor people's varied journeys

Respect people's time by starting and ending on time

Speak from your own experience and honor others'

Acknowledge intent, address impact

Accept and expect discomfort

Assume the best of one another

Take space, make space

Work to ask questions

*Interrupt attempts to derail and
keep the focus on the topic at hand*

Keep love (which is not always comfortable) as the goal

*Practice accountability
(the process by which someone who has committed harm
owns up to that harm and takes action to repair it)*

Express appreciation

Prioritize relationship over actions/goals

Collective action and collective leadership

We discuss and practice these values and agreements every time we gather; this is a commitment that builds muscle memory for how we want to be together. These lists are not static or complete and will be updated as we learn and grow.

Ok, we don't want to call the police. Now what?

Of course, there are communities for whom calling the police has never even seemed like a viable option—Black and Brown, undocumented, unhoused, poor and working class white, and queer communities, to name a few. We are grateful to organizations like the Black Panthers, the Brown Berets, the Audre Lorde Project, Communities United Against Violence, Critical Resistance, POOR Magazine/ Homefulness, the Anti Police-Terror Project, Community Ready Corps, and so many more who have, out of necessity, developed the skills we need. It is to these groups that we have turned for training.

Between January 2019 and this writing, we have offered eight Sunday afternoon trainings attended by anywhere from fifty to 175 people. Whenever possible, we chose and paid people of color to lead these trainings; we also took a collection most months for one of our local Black- or Indigenous-led organizations working toward police and prison abolition. The trainings we have hosted to date are:

- *White Supremacy and the State*—An overview of the history of white supremacy in the United States that aimed to put policing in a larger context of institutional racism.[6]

- *"Morality," Christian Supremacy, and the History of Policing*—Looking at the particular culpability of Christian institutions and ideology in creating our current criminal (in)justice system using excerpts from two Showing Up for Racial Justice webinars.[7]

- *White Supremacy Culture*—A discussion of Tema Okun's article[8] in the hope that we could be on alert for ways we might inadvertently replicate white supremacy in alternatives we discussed.

- *Transformative Justice*—How can we address harm in ways that don't invite or replicate state violence?[9]

- *Verbal De-escalation 101*—With a special focus on how to support people in mental health crisis.[10]

- *Self and Community Defense: Crisis Intervention and De-escalation*—More training in de-escalation and what to do if escalation happens anyway.[11]

- *Health Emergencies, First Aid, and CPR*—Including Narcan administration for opioid overdose.[12]

- *How to Not Call the Cops, Ever*—Led by the Homefulness/ POOR Magazine community, a group of unhoused, formerly unhoused, and housing insecure people who have lived and worked in community for twenty years without calling the police on anyone despite intense levels of trauma in their community.[13]

Deepening our skills and getting clear on our values prepared us to begin to incarnate another approach to community safety in several situations:

- We provided community security for the Jewish High Holy Days services of one of our member organizations.

- We took part in community security for Moms4Housing, a group of Black homeless mothers who took over a corporate-owned, long-vacant home in order to bring attention to the housing crisis in Oakland.

- When racist threats emerged against a city-sponsored antiracism lecture scheduled to take place at First Congregational Church of Oakland, we successfully organized to have a trusted community and movement security organization (Community Ready Corps) on duty instead of the Oakland Police Department.

Because most of our member organizations are predominantly white, and the planning team is predominantly white, our events have tended to draw mostly white participants from our circles. We have struggled with whether or not this is okay. On the one hand, we feel that dismantling white supremacy is white people's responsibility and that helping white people not call the police is vital; on the other, we want to make sure we are being accountable to those most impacted by policing. To date, that has mostly happened through personal relationships some of us have with leaders of color and through signal-boosting and supporting the demands and analysis of Black, Indigenous, and people of color (BIPOC) organizations. As the work continues, we would like to formalize relationships of accountability in some way.

We recognize that our ability to incarnate *these particular alternatives* is a benefit of living in a place like Oakland, with its rich legacy of people's movements; not everyone has access to these sorts of trainings. We also recognize that there are situations for which even a well-trained group is ill-prepared and might have to call the police—this is not a failing of that group but of our public infrastructure. Because we currently lack publicly funded community alternatives, we also emphasize the need for everyone to be trained as a cop watcher so that when the police *are* called, someone will be documenting what they do.

WE TRIED SOME THINGS—NOW WHAT?

Here are a few of the things we have learned along the way.

It's really all about relationship. In middle-class white American culture, we use the police as a way of avoiding relationship with those who make us uncomfortable, whether because they remind us of our racial shame or because they are behaving in ways we experience as loud or erratic or because we don't know how to set and maintain boundaries. The police are a shortcut we take to avoid the discomfort of having hard conversations, facing our racial realities, and learning new relational skills. The only alternative to policing, for real, is relationship.

White-middle-class understandings of "safety" are unrealistic. We live in these vulnerable, squishy bodies, and to remove all threat of harm to them is unrealistic. Black and Brown people have lived with this reality from the beginning of this country. Too often, white people mistake "safety" for "comfort," and we think of safety in terms of individuals, not communities. There is some level of embodied risk and discomfort in this work because we are no longer outsourcing both to policing. Christ is the model of God-become-vulnerable; to follow Christ's example is to become vulnerable for the sake of each other.

This is lifegiving work! Many of us, especially those of us with some relationship to white womanhood, have been encouraged by white supremacy and patriarchy to outsource our ability to take care of ourselves to armed men, and this has done us a tremendous disservice. It has made us vulnerable to abuse by those men, and it has separated us from our own power. Many of us found self- and community-defense trainings to be empowering and liberating, as well as challenging to our so-called niceness and politeness patterns.

The specter of sexual violence is the most frequently deployed argument against divesting from policing. So many people have asked us "What if someone is raped here?" despite the facts that police and the court system have an abysmal track record of dealing with sexual assault, that most sexual assault involves people who know each other, and that many people never report these experiences for these and a host of other reasons.[14]

Accountability is unbelievably rare in American society despite our love affair with punishment. Without accountability, we won't ever access even the modicum of safety that is realistic in the world.

Engaging with this material is hard on participants' nervous systems! We found it difficult to stay engaged for four-hour workshops. We plan to limit future workshops to three hours, to build in relationship-building and journaling/reflecting time, to incorporate generative somatics,[15] and to seek additional advice on how to make these trainings "trauma-informed." We join with people like Resmaa Menakem, author of My Grandmother's Hands, who are emphasizing the centrality of trauma healing in racial justice efforts.

THEN EVERYTHING CHANGED—NOW WHAT?

We were gearing up for a second round of trainings in 2020 when the COVID-19 pandemic hit, and all in-person events had to be canceled. Then, as we tried to figure out whether this work could happen online (much is lost when we can't sense each other's bodies), George Floyd was brutally murdered by Minneapolis police, and suddenly the work we and so many others had been doing, once fringe, was becoming mainstream. #DefundPolice started trending and generating mainstream media headlines and public debate.

In this incredible moment—the fruit of generations of Black, Brown, and Indigenous organizing—it has felt important, as a predominantly white group, to focus on amplifying the demands, trainings, and webinars of our BIPOC-led partners. We have finally created a Facebook page (@AlternativesToPolicingEastBay) where we are posting those offerings and calls to action, and we are also using our email list to spread the word.

In the summer of 2020, we also hosted an online organizing meeting to get our base to start organizing their own neighborhoods, faith communities, and organizations, in ways that will reduce reliance on policing in the future. Since then, our monthly meetings have provided accountability and support for doing that organizing work, which has taken the form of neighborhood meetings, altar creation, and socially distanced and online community building circles among members and/or neighbors.

We realize that our situation here in Oakland—a larger city full of communities and organizations with deep knowledge and practices around not calling the police—is not the situation for everybody. Fortunately, in terms of skill-building, there are vast archives of online webinars and trainings available.[16] The most important part of all this, however, is something that can be done in any community:

building relationships in which we can hold ourselves accountable to one another.

First Congo did eventually get that Black Lives Matter banner hung, but we are still working to incarnate what the phrase might mean. We are still on that journey. The details of our destination remain hazy, but having stepped out on this path, we know there is no going back. We are grateful to be together with our neighbors as we walk out into an unknown future.

BIBLE BLUEPRINT: Matthew 5: 21–26, 1 Corinthians 6: 1–8

Scripture is full of accounts of people organizing alternative ways of being in relationship that don't rely on or replicate the violence the empire inflicts. Just two examples include Jesus and Paul encouraging alternative accountability practices that avoid the Roman courts and prisons of their time. The communities they were trying to build — communities that centered collective well-being through such practices as sharing food and housing, and democratizing access to care for bodies — are thus intended to counter the impacts and practices of Roman colonization, which included the kind of policing of behavior and bodies described in this chapter. —Anne Dunlap

Notes

1. Lynice M. Pinkard, "Embracing Love's Ugly Baby," First Congregational Church of Oakland Christmas Eve Service, sermon, December 25, 2017, Oakland, California.

2. First Congregational Church of Oakland, "No More State-Sponsored Crucifixions in the Name of 'Safety,'" Google Doc, March 30, 2018, docs.google.com /document/d/1h-N2S8hKnIHdnlxvLp3oneym8c3GGzgQdUCOmMDNYMU /edit? usp=sharing.

3. "Invitation to Prophetic Imagination: Community Safety for All: Congregational Action Toolkit a Project of SURJ-Faith," Showing Up for Racial Justice–SURJ, https://surj.org/our-work/surj-faith/cs4a/.

4. Settler colonialism is a form of domination and exploitation that involves one group of people moving into the land or territory of another with the intention of subjugating or replacing the original inhabitants. Here in the Bay Area, this shows up in both historical and present-day genocide committed by white settlers on the Ohlone people, but also in gentrification. In terms of policing and safety, the values of settler colonialism undergird thinking about who "belongs" in a certain place and who is entitled to safety and necessities.

5. Sonya Renee Taylor, "Community Agreements," *The Body Is Not an Apology*, thebodyisnotanapology.com/about-tbinaa/community-agreements/.

6. Facilitated by Rev. Lynice Pinkard and Nichola Torbett.

7. We used excerpts from the following two excellent webinars: Andrea Ritchie, "Connecting the Dots: A History of Policing," Showing Up for Racial Justice, tinyurl.com/historyofpolicingwebinar; Yaz Nuñez and Alba Onofrio, "The Snatch Back," Showing Up for Racial Justice and Soulforce, tinyurl.com /sabotagechristiansupremacy.

8. Okun, "White Supremacy Culture: Characteristics."

9. Facilitated by the Bay Area Transformative Justice Collective, https://batjc .wordpress.com.

10. Facilitated by Elliott Fukui, madqueer.org.

11. Facilitated by Community Ready Corps.

12. Facilitated by Oakland Power Projects, https://oaklandpowerprojects.org.

13. Wisdom from this workshop has since been published by Poor Press in a book: Tiny Gray-Garcia, Leroy F. Moore, Jr., Jeremy Miller, Joey Villarreal, Muteado Silencio, Aunti Frances Moore, et al., *How Not to Call the Po'Lice Ever* (Oakland: Poor Press, 2020).

14. According to the Rape, Abuse, and Incest National Network (RAINN), out of every 1,000 sexual assaults, only 310 are reported to police, only fifty lead to arrest, and only twenty-five will result in incarceration. On the list of reasons why victims of sexual assault do not report to the police, the second highest was the belief that police "would not do anything." "The Criminal Justice System: Statistics," *RAINN*, www.rainn.org/statistics/criminal-justice-system. RAINN also reports that roughly eight out of every ten sexual assaults are committed by someone known to the victim, with fully one-third committed by a current or former significant other. "Perpetrators of Sexual Violence: Statistics," RAINN, www.rainn .org/statistics/perpetrators-sexual-violence. Finally, reporting at all is particularly difficult for victims of police sexual misconduct, who have no one to report to other than the police. A 2015 Associated Press investigation into police sexual misconduct revealed that nearly 1,000 officers in the United States lost their

badges due to sexual misconduct in the six-year period studied. This is only the tip of the iceberg of a nationwide problem, given underreporting and the limitations of the study. Matt Sedensky, "AP: Hundreds of Officers Lose Licenses over Sex Misconduct," *AP NEWS*, November 1, 2015, apnews.com/article/oklahoma-police-archive-oklahoma-city-fd1d4d05e561462a85abe50e7eaed4ec.

15. See Generative Somatics, https://generativesomatics.org/.

16. For example: Justice Teams Network "We Take Care of Us" series: https://justiceteams.org/wetakecareofus-webinar-series; SURJ's "Connecting the Dots" political education series: https://surj.org/category/past-webinars/; and SURJ-Faith's "Community Safety for All" toolkit: https://surj.org/our-work/surj-faith/cs4a/.

13

. . .

JOINING THE SANCTUARY MOVEMENT

. . .

NOEL ANDERSON

To the God of Peace, I pray for my children to be healthy and happy.
I pray for the freedom to watch them grow up,
To play with them,
To teach them to be respectful and kind,
To be sure they understand that everyone is equal and
That they are no better or worse than anyone else.
I pray to be able to live without fear,
And not under the gaze of people who are curious or feeling sorry for me.
I pray for the freedom to work to support my family,
To be part of a community,
And to live as other families live.
I pray that I will not worry about my future. Amen.

—Alex Garcia, Sanctuary leader from Christ Church UCC,
   Maplewood, MO[1]

Who wants to live in a church? Sometimes there is no other choice. If you were faced with the possibility of Immigration Customs Enforcement (ICE) coming to your house and ripping you away from your spouse and children, what would you do?

As one of the national leaders in the Sanctuary Movement efforts, and as a UCC ordained minister, I work with many people facing this very question. Becoming a part of the Sanctuary Movement is just one way people of faith can take part in faith-rooted organizing to stop deportations, win immigrants' rights, and make an impact in the broader struggle for racial justice in the United States.

My own story as an ally for immigrant and refugee justice began as my family, when I was a young child, moved from town to town for my father's occupation as a United Methodist pastor. We were most often in small rural farm towns, and the children of immigrants were always first to befriend and welcome me as the new kid. I spent several years living and working in Central America's Northern Triangle,[2] where I learned about the root causes of migration and the history of colonialism and military intervention from the United States. Knowing the ties of the Central American reality to forced migration, I became involved in the Sanctuary efforts to stop deportations in 2007 while in seminary, during the mass raids of the Bush administration. As a person of faith, I believe we have a moral obligation to confront these unjust immigration laws and even defy them in order to keep families together. As a father, I cannot imagine having my son taken from me, or being forcibly removed from his life, or my wife's, due to detention or deportation.

The current need for the Sanctuary Movement rises out of the United States' unjust immigration system, which is tearing families and communities apart. Military intervention and trade agreements have forced migrants to the United States for generations; immigration rules make it difficult to impossible for millions to adjust their status.[3] Criminalization of migrants and mass deportations have become a norm. Under former President Obama, there were daily detentions of approximately 35,000 people, totaling over five million deportations.[4] The trend deepened with former President Trump's hateful rhetoric and the administration's harmful policies, including family separation at the border and the attempt to shut down asylum, refugee resettlement, Deferred Action for Childhood Arrival (DACA), family sponsorship, and Temporary Protected Status, all of which has impacted millions of immigrants across the country.[5]

Although today President Biden has created relief from deportation for many people claiming sanctuary, his administration has continued the pattern of mass deportations by keeping many Trump policies in place, such as the misuse of the Title 42 health code, which has been utilized during the pandemic to block asylum at the border and expel hundreds of thousands of asylum seekers. Haitians and Africans at the border are experiencing anti-Black discrimination by other migrants, and when attempting to claim asylum, they face institutional racism by both Mexican and US officials. By May 2021, President Biden had deported or expelled nearly 500,000 people, as his administration continued to implement policies influenced by the ongoing politicization of this issue. The Republican party, heavily influenced by former President Trump, has led a political strategy that utilizes immigration to stoke fear and incite a sense of white nationalism, while using border security and militarization as leverage. The Governor of Texas, Gregg Abbot, has now criminalized asylum seekers crossing through the desert[6] and even attempted to blame them for the rise in COVID cases,[7] even though he failed to implement mask-wearing policies or implement robust vaccination efforts himself.[8]

The need for faith communities to take action on immigration has continued its urgency across different presidential administrations and will only grow as more people are displaced by climate change, increased natural disasters, and political destabilization.

This chapter will offer a brief overview of the Sanctuary Movement, give practical strategies for how to become a Sanctuary Congregation, and share learnings through excerpts of interviews with migrants, undocumented people, asylum seekers, and the faith community allies who accompany them within the Sanctuary Movement. These stories highlight how brave immigrant leaders confront the unjust laws of our nation, how faith communities are taking bold actions in solidarity, and how transformational change occurs within our congregations as a result.

WHAT IS THE SANCTUARY MOVEMENT AND SANCTUARY?

Our organization defines sanctuary in three ways: The most important aspect is advocacy - pushing back on harsh laws and federal policies and carving out spaces for families to survive and stay together. The second is accompaniment, a direct encounter and experience accompanying a long-term resident family under threat of deportation - in their own campaign, or a newly arrived family also fighting deportation in their struggle to get legal help, to settle, to stabilize enough to get their bearings and get due process and life. The third is congregational housing, congregations and individuals from congregations providing housing hospitality.

Rev. Deborah Lee, UCC Pastor and
Executive Director of Interfaith
Movement for Human Integrity, CA[9]

The Sanctuary Movement, as we understand it within a modern context, began in the 1980s as a result of Cold War politics in Central American countries, which caused thousands of refugees to flee civil war and seek asylum. The US government refused to recognize them as political refugees, even though they were fleeing government sanctioned death squads. Congregations on the southern US border started taking in thousands of people and created an underground network of churches throughout the country that helped cross, house, and resettle people. This was a very prophetic act because of its confrontation with US policies meant to criminalize undocumented people and allies who shelter and aid them.[10] Together with strong immigrant Central American voices, faith communities advocated to win refugee status for people fleeing, ensure Temporary Protective Status, and end US funding of civil wars in Central America.[11]

The Sanctuary Movement today is a national effort to bring together congregations and immigrant leaders to build collective power and lift prophetic voices in order to shift the public narrative through advocacy, accompaniment, and housing. Through the Sanctuary Movement, faith communities in particular can enact and embody their commitment to justice, creating a dramatic tension that forces the public and elected officials to question the morality of our immigration policies. The number of Sanctuary Congregations has increased in the last several years from 400 to 1,200 congregations nationwide as the need has risen with increased political attacks against immigrants. A congregation that declares itself a Sanctuary Congregation is one that is willing to engage in a spectrum of solidarity actions including welcoming undocumented people, advocating to help stop deportations, assisting with legal clinics, and physically sheltering an immigrant in danger of immediate deportation.[12]

People facing deportation can seek viable shelter in a house of worship because ICE has a policy that they will not enforce immigration in a house of worship. But since it is their own policy, they could choose to violate it, as they have when it comes to other sensitive locations such as schools and hospitals. The legality of Sanctuary is a common question. If a congregation works to launch a public case, then they are not "shielding from detention" or "concealing" anyone. However, this is a legal grey area that is up to lawyers and courts' interpretations of harboring statutes.[13] What is clear is that immigrant leaders and faith communities are confronting these unjust laws and deportation policies publicly by declaring that these families should stay united and that individuals should not be ripped from their homes and communities. Not every case is a public Sanctuary case, as many immigrant leaders prefer their story to not be told in the public sphere in order to protect loved ones.

Sanctuary is rooted in faith, sacred texts, and prophetic witness in response to the need that arises in the community to keep families together. Again and again, the Hebrew Bible and Gospels remind us to love the stranger—for we were once strangers in the land of Egypt—and to care for marginalized populations and see the face of Christ in the stranger.

BECOMING A SANCTUARY CONGREGATION

Becoming a Sanctuary Congregation begins by educating your congregation and raising awareness about the pertinent issues through book and Bible studies, worship resources, webinars, community events, films, and documentaries. Pay attention to the root causes of migration, including the history of colonialism, US military and economic intervention, and the role of racial injustice and xenophobia. It is critical for key congregation members to develop authentic relationships of accompaniment and solidarity with impacted leaders by engaging community members, local immigrants' rights organizations, legal service providers, and workers rights groups. Congregations should take direct guidance and leadership from impacted community members themselves. One faith community should not try to take on the work of Sanctuary alone, but should instead mobilize a coalition or collaborative with other congregations and human rights groups, which includes creating a structure for volunteer roles. It is often helpful to create a public statement or covenant around becoming a Sanctuary Congregation that includes an institutional approval or congregational vote. Often, this can come with a public action, press conference, or vigil.

If there is a need for someone to claim physical sanctuary, there should be a period of discernment among the congregation, the person claiming sanctuary, their family, their lawyer, and any key volunteers and organizers. A congregation should determine if they have the right space to offer sanctuary, which is defined locally by the coalition and those leaders in need of sanctuary. If it is a public sanctuary case, it is often accompanied with a public launch event which includes centering the story of the Sanctuary Congregation leader and the importance of stopping their deportation. Non-public sanctuary cases are also common, and a good alternative for temporary needs or if someone does not feel comfortable sharing their story publicly.

The daily work of sustaining sanctuary is ongoing, including volunteers to help with basic needs: food, mental health, medical, legal services, advocacy, spiritual support, and continued events or actions to uplift the case. Fundraising is generally a critical component to ensure there are resources for these activities. Make sure to establish a system for management of funds raised ahead of time and, in doing so, center immigrant Sanctuary Movement leaders in the decision-making process (see chapter 14). For more resources and a step-by-step toolkit on becoming a Sanctuary Congregation, see the Sanctuary Not Deportation website.[14]

CHOOSING SANCTUARY FOR HOUSING

Minerva Cisneros Garcia, a mother of three in Winston-Salem, North Carolina, came to the United States to find a better school for her blind son, Eduardo, who was five years old at the time. Seventeen years later she entered sanctuary. The prosecutorial discretion guidelines under the Obama Administration that allowed thousands of immigrants to continue living in the United States under a stay of removal were thrown out under Trump, leaving people like Minerva, who had been checking in with ICE for ten years, with no other choice but to seek sanctuary in order to keep her family together.

> The reason I moved here is to ensure education for my son Eduardo, who is blind, because in Mexico, there were no special education programs for him like there are here in the U.S. We had previously received humanitarian relief from deportation, but when President Trump came into office, everything changed, and they said we had to leave and go back to Mexico, but if I left and brought my son who is a DACA recipient, he may never be able to return to the US. I decided to enter Sanctuary to be able to see if I could keep fighting my case to stay here with my children. So I went to the church to see how to resolve this problem and they opened their doors and welcomed me.
>
> Minerva Cisneros Garcia,
> Winston-Salem, North Carolina[15]

Minerva was one of the first people to claim sanctuary in North Carolina and after months of living in Congregational UCC Greensboro, a judge finally ruled in her favor, allowing her to eventually adjust her status and become a citizen. This was a huge victory. Minerva described it as the best day of her life.

> There are a lot of logistics involved in becoming a Sanctuary Congregation. We started learning by asking all the tough questions. Ultimately when we met Minerva and learned of her story, it was a total consensus; people said 'how could we not?' Minerva's presence really was a blessing in many ways for us. It was an unusual thing to hold together the suffering

of this woman and her family, and all of us knowing we could walk out these doors at any time and she couldn't. So there was this great sorrow knowing how much she was giving up to be here, and at the same time, tremendous blessing. Her presence focused our congregation like nothing else has ever focused us. It was hard work, but work that we loved, and we all fell in love with this family.

Rev. Julie Peeples, Greensboro
Community Congregational, NC[16]

Although this is an incredible success story, sanctuary can be extremely challenging. The rise of hate and discrimination against immigrants continues to be provoked by harmful political rhetoric from all levels of leadership. Its combination with harsh policies has led to an increase in detentions and deportations. Many people who are claiming sanctuary are forced to stay under the protection of a house of worship for years of continued denials of a stay of removal[17] while trying to adjust their immigration status. Enduring and sustaining through the many hardships and challenges, the resources, time, and money spent, countless losses and few wins, requires a constant renewal of faith.

LEARNINGS FROM SANCTUARY

Without fail, both the congregation and the family claiming sanctuary find themselves on a new spiritual journey. It is a life changing experience for all who participate. The act of coming together for a just cause is never easy. It is hard work and there are often many difficult complications or conflicts that arise. It's important for people to learn from these challenges as they work together towards transformation.

Alex has transformed us as individuals and as a congregation. For some who were against allowing him to come, they are some of the ones closest to him, who love him most and would do anything in the world for him and the feeling is mutual.

Rev. Rebecca Turner, Christ
Church, Maplewood, Missouri[18]

God is not a building, God is something much larger than that. The community support is very important; we need others to mobilize, we need white allies to turn out. The people of faith are incredible, they often put forward their bodies. They help us with our spiritual lives, Jericho walks and vigils, these actions are very important.

Jeanette Vizguerra, Co-Founder,
Metro Denver Sanctuary Coalition[19]

The prayer that opens this chapter was written for the UCC National Day of Prayer by Alex Garcia, who migrated from Honduras to escape violence. Nearly fifteen years after settling in the United States with his wife, his job, and five kids who are US citizens, he was placed under imminent threat of deportation. When Alex needed a place to go, Christ Church UCC in Maplewood, Missouri answered the call to keep his family together.

For me, Sanctuary has shown me how important my family is for me. When I think about what could happen tomorrow, the weight of deportation…It has been difficult because we try one thing in our campaign to win freedom, but it feels like we are often hitting a wall. What keeps giving me hope is to keep with my family, that a miracle might happen, the moment where I can go free with my family.

Rev. Alex Garcia, Christ Church,
Maplewood, Missouri[20]

Many congregations join Sanctuary efforts from a sense of charity, but soon are forced to learn the skills of actual community organizing as they recognize that commitments towards liberation and freedom demand a strategic campaign with an arch of escalating tactics that can create dramatic tension and gain increased attention from decision makers. It is one thing to condemn the act of family separation, but to actually put a faith community between ICE and the family in danger of deportation requires a level of faith that involves risk (see chapter 4).

> Sanctuary at first is about charity, but as time dragged on, the entire congregation eventually understood providing Sanctuary is not about room and board, it has to include Alex's freedom, it has to include real advocacy with politicians, policy makers, ICE officials and with anyone who has the power to change Alex's situation. This carries over significantly in all of our work in the community.
>
> Rev. Rebecca Turner, Christ
> Church, Maplewood, Missouri[21]

The Sanctuary Movement is not linked to a single organization, faith tradition, or denomination, but instead moves across grassroots networks, coalitions, and collectives. It is an organic movement of people of faith across congregations, impacted leaders, and immigrants' rights and/or civil rights organizations in which people coordinate and organize themselves according to local or regional strategies and needs. Many denominations have their own organizing structures, such as the United Church of Christ National Collaborative on Immigration, a group of grassroots pastors and lay leaders that helped pass a General Synod Resolution in 2017 declaring the denomination Immigrant Welcoming. Many Immigrant Welcoming Congregations are also Sanctuary Congregations.[22] Other denominations are moving forward in similar ways, such as the Evangelical Lutheran Church of America, which declared itself a Sanctuary Denomination in 2019.[23] Broadening out, many have embraced Sanctuary City campaigns to help disentangle local police from arresting and detaining people for ICE.[24]

There is an overarching national strategy around stopping deportations and building collective power to effectuate long-term sustainable changes in the unjust and oppressive immigration system. Presently, though, each person claiming sanctuary is forced to concentrate on the necessary steps to keep up the everyday struggle to win their case and have some type of relief from deportation. If we can win just one case at a time, we can build momentum towards greater change in the broader system. Those who have gained temporary relief from deportation often continue to collaborate with faith communities to set forth the broader struggle for immigrants' rights.

> For us it was a transformative experience, it was hard work, it involved lots of volunteers and congregations. It helped us to make stronger connections to understand more about racial injustice, seeing it firsthand, understanding more about what was happening with DHS and ICE. It was a time of tremendous learning, to center the immigrant voices and their experiences, that it wasn't about us, but about them.
>
> Rev. Julie Peeples, Greensboro
> Community Congregational, NC[25]

ADDRESSING WHITE PRIVILEGE AND WORKING TOWARDS RACIAL JUSTICE

> It is crystal clear that racism is at the heart of the attacks on immigrants and refugees. ICE is not going to target people who look like most of us in our congregation. It really is very connected to the history of white supremacy and racism.
>
> Rev. Julie Peeples, Greensboro
> Community Congregational, NC[26]

Anti-immigrant rhetoric and the politics of fear have made it clear that the constant attack on immigrants is not merely focused on legality. Rather, it is driven by discrimination against skin color, accent, and culture. At the root of xenophobic policies is racism and the attempt to limit the increasingly diverse landscape of American culture.

White supremacy culture, the widespread ideology that whiteness is superior to BIPOC, Muslim people, or immigrants, permeates US faith communities and the way in which these religious institutions function.[27] Predominantly white congregations have members who are accustomed to the white privilege they experience through normalized societal and institutional advantages. One manifestation of this in the Christian tradition is the theology of white saviorism, which allows white people to occupy the hero role and, in doing so, disempower marginalized communities who are being targeted. Even when congregational volunteers are conscious of unequal power dynamics, small problems can grow unless there is an understanding of how white privilege functions in the everyday reality with clear communication channels to mitigate tensions.

> The biggest problem we have is white allies from the congregation wanting to save us, they don't understand that we ourselves are the agents of our own liberation. The churches have to learn that families are very vulnerable, and they sometimes make it seem like they will take away their support and protection if [families] don't listen to the opinion or the direction the congregation suggests. We should listen to the families first, and not use the privileges of the church to control things.
>
> Jeanette Vizguerra, Co-Founder,
> Metro Denver Sanctuary Coalition[28]

In order for white people to not fall into the patterns of white saviorism, it is important to get behind and follow impacted leaders who are agents of the change they desire to see in the world. One concrete way this plays out in the work of sanctuary is through decision-making structures. There is a tendency to look to experts, such as lawyers, pastors, and advocates, to make decisions about a particular situation. Instead, those who are impacted—those who are claiming sanctuary—should have the final decision about when and how to take sanctuary, how to move the arch of escalation on the campaign, what the exit strategy should be, and how to manage funds raised.

> We have really tried to emphasize the leadership of those directly impacted. They are the ones leading their campaigns, their journey. It is their lives. It does take considerable "untraining" of volunteers and accompaniment teams to be constantly checking their own assumptions and tendencies.
>
> Rev. Deborah Lee, UCC Pastor and
> Executive Director of Interfaith
> Movement for Human Integrity, CA[29]

Born out of the needs that arise in the community, affected leaders must always be at the center of the work. The decision to claim sanctuary is not made by activists, the congregation, nor the pastor; that decision lies with the undocumented families themselves. The role of the congregation is to support, accompany, and walk alongside impacted leaders.

> It is key to think about sanctuary and immigrant rights as racial justice movements. Not everyone thinks of it this way, but if we don't address immigration policy as an expression of White supremacy and racism, we will completely miss the boat. We must also see sanctuary as resistance to policies of criminalization.
>
> Rev. Deborah Lee, UCC Pastor and
> Executive Director of Interfaith
> Movement for Human Integrity, CA[30]

SANCTUARY AS ACCOMPANIMENT

Sanctuary is broader than just physical shelter in a house of worship and extends to asylum seekers and refugees in need of accompaniment. Many Sanctuary Congregations help people get released from detention, or assist in stopping a deportation, without ever needing to claim sanctuary within a house of worship.

Terry Rombot is an Indonesian asylum seeker who became undocumented after his case for asylum was denied. He is a leader at Maranatha Indonesian UCC in Madbury, New Hampshire. On two different occasions, a judge ruled that he would be eligible to stay in the country, yet ICE picked up Terry anyway. As he sat on the plane ready to be deported back to Indonesia, ICE suddenly let him call his Pastor, Rev. Sandra Pontoh. She rallied people, including a pastor of Reformed Church of Highland Park, New Jersey, Rev. Seth Kaper-Dale, and the churches started mobilizing and making calls to ICE. At the last minute, Terry was taken off the plane and spared deportation just before it took off.

At the time of writing this, over fifty Indonesians have won their asylum cases over the last three years and dozens more, including Terry, are still waiting for their cases to be heard. Because of the organizing efforts in New Hampshire and New Jersey, hundreds of Indonesians avoided deportations and family separation.

> ICE transferred me from one jail to the next, almost every jail, I've been there. I don't think many people could face that, but God helped me, and God gave me strength. I realized that miracles are real, it happens. Without this miracle, I wouldn't be here today. I hope people can learn from my story and have strong faith.
>
> Terry Rombot, Maranatha Indonesian
> UCC, Madbury, New Hampshire[31]

Terry Rombot and Rev. Sandra Pontoh emphasized the importance of organizing the surrounding congregations in New Hampshire, New Jersey, and Boston, and the work even garnered attention from Associate General Minister, Rev. Traci Blackmon and General Minister and President, Rev. John Dorhauer of the United Church of Christ. The various congregations, coalitions, and networks helped build power to ensure Terry and others were not deported. Rev. Pontoh expressed her emotions about being an immigrant-led congregation that received such support:

> I feel like the faith community and the church is not giving up on us (Indonesian asylum seekers), and that means so much, to provide hope and inspiration to keep fighting. It makes us feel safe. We don't feel alone any longer, in the past I cried, we were the youngest church here, but we didn't have anyone. I remember that, it was so tough, because I felt alone, but now I can call so many people around the country who will support us. We are welcome. I can't expect people to know what's going on without saying anything. I can't expect people to reach out to my community, until I speak up.
>
> Rev. Sandra Pontoh, Pastor of
> Maranatha Indonesian UCC,
> Madbury, New Hampshire[32]

NEED FOR PROPHETIC ACTION

Unfortunately, state violence against immigrants will continue to be a part of US politics for the foreseeable future. The role of faith communities to be a prophetic voice and moral compass is critical for making change in leadership and policies at the local, state, and federal levels. As people of faith, we cannot simply quote our sacred texts and talk about what is the moral imperative; we must live out our faith and take action. This means accompaniment and lifting up the stories of impacted leaders, changing the public narrative, assisting in leadership development, joining actions led by immigrants themselves, and holding our decision makers accountable. Congregations who participate in these activities find that their mission and purpose is being fulfilled, which strengthens the vitality of their faith community. We are called by faith to join the broader fight for immigrant rights and racial justice as part of the many issues that impact our communities.

> We have an ethical responsibility to stand up to these unjust immigration laws because we follow a higher law, to love our neighbors. This is Sanctuary for everyone, and it means that everyone is going to need to see how these issues—no, ALL issues—are connected. When impacted communities start organizing together, joined by allies in the faith community, we can build power at the local level to make the concrete changes needed to protect marginalized communities.

> Rev. Juliean DeShazier, Senior Pastor at
> University Church, Chicago, Illinois[33]

BIBLE BLUEPRINT: Exodus 22:21

"You shall not wrong or oppress a migrant, for you were migrants in the land of Egypt" (NRSV, adapted). God's concern for the migrant (*ger* in biblical Hebrew means "stranger," "sojourner," or "foreigner" and in context is close in meaning to migrant or immigrant) is found a multitude of times throughout the Bible. Migrants are centered as a primary concern, along with widows and orphans, for care and for justice; a thriving community has to include the wellbeing of the migrants. God reminds God's people that they were also migrants: people move, it's what we do. We wander, we move with the seasons, we seek out better shelter and soil. And sometimes, we are stolen from our land, our land and our livelihood are stolen from us, our safety is stolen from us, and we must flee. God is clear that we must protect one another for all the reasons we move, and most especially when we flee. Church as sanctuary is rooted in this care and protection for one another. —*Anne Dunlap*

Notes

1. Alex Garcia, "Interfaith Day of Prayer," United Church of Christ, May, 2020, https://www.ucc.org/worship-way/idop_alex_garcia_5_7_2020/.

2. The "Northern Triangle" is a term used by the United States for Guatemala, Honduras, and El Salvador. It is one of the poorest regions in the western hemisphere.

3. To adjust status means to change from undocumented to documented immigration status, or to change from one kind of immigration status, such as a visa, to another, such as a residency permit or "green card."

4. Muzaffar Chishti and Sarah Pierce Muzaffar Chishti, "The Obama Record on Deportations: Deporter in Chief or Not?" Migrationpolicy.org, August 2, 2019, www.migrationpolicy.org/article/obama-record-deportations-deporter-chief-or-not.

5. Michael D. Shear and Miriam Jordan, "Undoing Trump's Anti-immigrant Policies Will Mean Looking at the Fine Print," *New York Times*, February 10, 2021, https://www.nytimes.com/2021/02/10/us/politics/trump-biden-us-immigration-system.html.

6. Jolie McCullough, "The First Migrants Arrested in Gov. Greg Abbott's Border Crackdown Have Served Their Time. Federal Officials Will Decide What Happens Next," *The Texas Tribune*, August 11, 2021, https://www.texastribune.org/2021/08/11/texas-immigration-jail-abbott/.

7. Elizabeth Thompson and Alfredo Corchado, "Gov. Abbott Blames Immigrants for Spreading Covid in Rhetoric That Advocates Dismiss as Xenophobic," *Dallas Morning News*, March 4, 2021, https://www.dallasnews.com/new s/politics/2021/03/05/gov-abbott-blames-immigrants-for-spreading-covid-in-what-advocates-dismiss-as-rhetoric-at-its-best/.

8. Robert T. Garrett and Allie Morris, "Gov. Greg Abbott Says No Texas Business Can Force Employees to Take Covid-19 Vaccine," *Dallas Morning News*, October 12, 2021, https://www.dallasnews.com/news/politics/2021/10/11/gov-greg-abbott-says-no-texas-business-can-force-employee-to-take-covid-19-vaccine/.

9. Rev. Deborah Lee, "Questions for UCC Chapter." Email Received by Rev. Noel Andersen, August 2020. Email Interview.

10. See US legal code 8 U.S.C. § 1324(a)(1)(A)(iii).

11. Susan Gzesh, "Central Americans and Asylum Policy in the Reagan Era," *Migrationpolicy.org*, April 1, 2006, www.migrationpolicy.org/article/central-americans-and-asylum-policy-reagan-era.

12. Myrna Orozco and Noel Andersen, "Sanctuary in the Age of Trump," January 2018, https://www.sanctuarynotdeportation.org/sanctuary-report-2018.html.

13. See US legal code 8 U.S.C. § 1324(a)(1)(A)(iii). See also American Civil Liberties Union, "Sanctuary Congregations and Harboring, FAQ," April 13, 2017.

14. Sanctuary Not Deportation (including Interfaith Sanctuary Toolkit), http://sanctuarynotdeportation.org/.

15. Minerva Garcia, Interview by Rev. Noel Andersen, December 2020.

16. Rev. Julie Peeples, Interview by Rev. Noel Andersen, September 2020.

17. A stay of removal is an immigration court order that someone not be deported.

18. Rev. Rebecca Turner, Interview byRev. Noel Andersen, August 2020.

19. Jeanette Vizguerra, Interview by Rev. Noel Andersen, August 2020.

20. Alex Garcia, Interview by Rev. Noel Andersen, August–September 2020.

21. Turner interview.

22. United Church of Christ Immigration Resources, https://www.ucc.org/justice_immigration/.

23. Evangelical Lutheran Church in America, "Sanctuary Denomination," https://www.elca.org/sanctuarychurch.

24. Lena Graber and Nikki Marquez, "Searching for Sanctuary," Immigrant Legal Resource Center, December 2016, https://www.ilrc.org/sites/default/files/resources/sanctuary_report_final_1-min.pdf.

25. Peeples interview.

26. Peeples interview.

27. Tema Okun, White Supremacy Culture, https://www.whitesupremacyculture.info/.

28. Vizguerra interview.

29. Lee interview.

30. Lee interview.

31. Terry Rombot, Interview by Rev. Noel Andersen, August 2020.

32. Rev. Sandra Pontoh, Interview by Rev. Noel Andersen, August 2020.

33. Rev. Julian DeShazier, "Building Sanctuary for All . . . All of Us," *United Church of Christ Witness for Justice*, May 3, 2017, https://www.ucc.org/building_sanctuary_for_all/.

14

. . .

LIVING INTO NEW SOLIDARITIES
Mutual Aid as Gospel Practice

. . .

MARGARET ERNST AND CATHY CARRILLO

Hoy por ti, mañana por mi.
—Latin American saying[1]

OUR JOURNEYS TOWARDS MUTUAL AID AND
FINDING EACH OTHER ALONG THE WAY

Cathy's Story

I am a first-generation US citizen, daughter to working-class undocumented Peruvian immigrants who came to the United States in 1995. I was raised in the Seventh-Day Adventist church, where the mentors and teachers I admired most encouraged me to search for meaning and understanding in a world that was full of boundaries and limitations. I was encouraged to develop a relationship with Christ and God that extended beyond the rules and regulations forced upon me.

On March 29, 2009, I witnessed first-hand the injustice of deportation that my family had always known and talked about, but never faced head-on. As I watched the state take away my father, I searched for the meaning and understanding of this moment. It wasn't until this crisis that I deeply understood the meaning of community. Long before definitions were available to me, I saw the difference between charity and mutual aid. Our church gave us charity. Our community gave us mutual aid.

My dad was a construction worker. He gave co-workers rides, and they would share their access to tools. It was a mutual exchange: other *compas* could get to work, and the tools meant my dad could get side jobs to keep making money for our family. When someone needed shelter, they stayed with us; in exchange, they would help with child-care. My dad would treat folks to meals or bring food for gatherings; he'd check in on folks, offering an extra hand moving, a box of nails, or playing a supporting role in an emergency. It was an informal but powerful understanding: when I help you, you help me too, and we both survive. My father and my community's actions reminded me, *Hoy por ti, mañana por mi*: Today for you, tomorrow for me.

When my dad was deported, our church helped. They asked us for our bills and simply paid off all of the remaining debt on the car note. They bought groceries they thought we would need and dropped them off at our door. And they provided rides to places we needed like work, legal appointments, or the grocery store.

But mutual aid came from the Peruvian community: *compas* who had worked alongside my father and people that he touched with his embodiment of mutual aid. They would ask us which tasks we needed help with, and supported us with what they could. When we had to move and needed storage, friends stored what they could. They noticed what would be harder for us with just one parent, picking us up on the way to work, soccer practice, or the store. Because they had faced similar situations, they knew that there would be things that we would miss, like home-cooked meals when we didn't have a kitchen for a while; they invited us to their homes or out to eat so we could feel a bit more normal. Our community gave to us because of the investment that my father made in other community members. I learned that the deep investment in relationship, community, and resource-building leads to the creation of something that can protect and guide us when all the systems that are meant to support us have failed.

I was drawn to put into practice my father's examples in 2016, when I became involved in Sanctuary organizing in Nashville. I was working for an immigration attorney, shedding light on the injustices that were happening to undocumented immigrants in Nashville and everywhere. I helped expose how the system criminalized my neighbors and loved ones. In this work I met Margaret and learned that the gospel calls us as believers to be engaged politically in this work. I went on to become a community defense organizer: organizing, defending, and advocating for the same immigrant community that had given me so much years before. In 2018, along with close friends and community members, I founded Movements Including X (The MIX). The MIX is a group of people who are like me: first-generation English speakers from mixed status[2] families who knew there was more we could do and build. We embody what we learned from our parents, from our ancestors, and our community: to take action, to protect and defend, and to unlearn and rebuild with each other.

Margaret's Story

I am descended from German, Scottish, and English immigrants who came to this continent over the past three centuries and whose whiteness granted access to land and economic opportunities as settlers. My father worked in corporate public relations for a company that encouraged my parents to move to one of the wealthiest zip codes in the country, where I was born: a Connecticut suburb with a notorious history of racism, classism, and antisemitism. Most of my friends' fathers were Wall Street bankers who made money for investors while gaining vast wealth of their own. Even with my dad's corporate income, I knew that we were looked down on because we didn't have as much money as others or live in a large house. I also knew how people, including at church, used words like "lucky," "fortunate," and "blessed" as code to describe being wealthy. My environment communicated, in every way, that people with more wealth were better people.

Changes in my family dramatically flipped our circumstances and how I saw the world. My dad came out as transgender when she was in her early sixties. The jobs she had access to as white and male were no longer possible. High-end public relations firms were not hiring older people and definitely not transwomen. After she came out, my dad was able to have the inner peace and contentment of being her true self. But even with her white privilege that protected her from even more extreme discrimination, she faced housing instability, joblessness, and physical violence. For the last years of her life she lived in poverty, relying on loans from friends and minimum wage work to scrape by. My mother did everything she could to maintain the comforts we grew up with. But our wealth and status had changed dramatically; I came to know personally the shame that comes in our society for needing help. I saw how wealth inequality dehumanizes those who have access to resources and those who don't, and I leaned on my faith to help me understand that my true worth and value were in God, not my social status.

True security is in community. The economy had granted me and my family our worth and value conditionally—when it was working for us. God's unconditional love stood in direct contrast to that conditionality. I learned through mutually supportive communities that blessing is having a community of mutual care and support—mutual aid!—that stands against values of greed and scarcity. These experiences pushed me into faith-based community organizing and ministry, focusing on racial and economic justice. I got to know Cathy when I helped to create a network of congregations offering solidarity and sanctuary for families facing detention and deportation in Nashville, where I was in divinity school. Building, strategizing, and creating community alongside working-class immigrants in Nashville taught me about lessons of courage, love, and radical hospitality that I will never forget and for which I am deeply grateful.

THEOLOGY AND PRINCIPLES OF MUTUAL AID

So, what *is* mutual aid? Mutual aid creates alternative structures of justice within an unjust system, modeling what is possible when we live through an ethic of sharing rather than scarcity. Based on our experience, we have identified four important core principles:

1. Mutual aid is mutually dignifying, challenging traditional binaries and hierarchies of giver and receiver.

2. People identify their own needs.

3. There is a path to leadership in decision-making about how aid is distributed.

4. Mutual aid puts people in relationship with each other, building collective consciousness of larger systems in order to build power to change them.

Though we were both raised Christian, neither of us learned about mutual aid from our churches. And yet, practicing mutual aid has taught us what lies at the heart of the gospel: mutual aid brings us back to basic human instincts *and* the initial vision of the church. Mutual aid is revolutionary yet ancient, deeply challenging yet innately human, all in one. But because of the way we internalize power, ideas about charity, the "deserving" or "undeserving" poor, racism, classism, and elitism, we have to retrain ourselves to return to our instincts of sharing and the gospel call of collective salvation.

Our impulse to share is our birthright: we see the children in our lives showing love for others by freely offering gifts to those around them: a toy, a book, a leaf off the ground. In the New Testament, we see descriptions of the disciples sharing "everything they had," an abolition of private property that would seem extremist to most churches and certainly to our government. Jesus tells his rich disciples on multiple occasions to sell their possessions and give the proceeds to people who need it.[3] The same principle is operating among the movement in Acts 4: Imagine! People with access to inherited wealth, land, and property sold it all and gave the profits to the movement to be distributed equally![4] Similarly, leaders in Jerusalem told Paul that he must collect money from the Gentiles, who had the privileges of Roman citizenship, for poor Jewish members of the Jerusalem *ekklesia*.[5] The sacraments point us towards what the Archbishop Rowan Williams calls "new solidarities" in Christ's saving love.[6] Williams points out that many of our relationships in society are marked by exploitation: the exploitation of workers by employers; of Indigenous peoples in Peru whose land is being polluted by pipeline CEOs and shareholders;[7] of tomato pickers in Florida working in unsafe conditions for consumers in Michigan. When we are baptized into the church, renouncing the powers of evil and receiving the freedom of new life in Christ,[8] we claim and are claimed within new kinds of relationships—relationships of justice, dignity, and mutual belovedness, new solidarities made possible in Christ. Mutual aid calls us into these new solidarities, which we are reminded of at the communion table when we remember that God sets a table for all, right here in the midst of public health crises, late capitalism, and the terrors of deportation, empire, white supremacy, and climate change.

To be clear, mutual aid is not charity. Charity reinforces an economic system designed for resources to flow to the few rather than the many. Charity redistributes just enough money to those the economy is devastating, exploiting, and dispossessing so that corporations and the uber-rich appear goodwilled and thus deserving of the power—and tax breaks!—they have. Charity is popular because it assuages the conscience of those who benefit from oppression. In the Roman Empire, in Jesus's time, it was considered a part of good Roman citizenship to give to the poor.[9] But charity, then and now, reinforces the economic status quo by ensuring that decision-making power remains in the hands of elites. This occurs through philanthropists, grant makers, and even churches, who set the terms for which people or organizations receive support, enforcing their own goals, values, and cultural norms.[10]

One of the imperial-cultural expectations of giving away resources is that the giver remains in control what is done with them. This mentality must change if we are to do mutual aid through a gospel lens. On multiple occasions in the New Testament, Jesus feeds people when others think there's not enough to go around. Turning water into wine, feeding a multitude with just five loaves and four fish, Jesus makes sure no one goes hungry. Meeting basic needs in a context in which elites controlled resources was a central part of his ministry of healing. But Jesus didn't feed people as an elite himself. He provided for others and demonstrated acts of radical sharing as someone who knew need and relied on the hospitality of others. His disciples were working people, like fishermen who had to survive on a day's wages. Jesus's social location reveals that the model of ministry into which he invited everyone was a ministry of mutual aid. We must ask ourselves what Jesus is really demanding of us when he says to "feed his sheep," and examine where the church has gotten the gospel call for transformation and healing confused with the dominant culture's value on charity.

Doing mutual aid in a "Jesus way" requires a reorientation away from how we are used to being in relationship with each other across our culture's dominant power dynamics. For people who experience the shame and stigma of struggling to cover basic needs, it's important to reclaim power and dignity and the right to be an agent of change, and to see one's worth and value through Jesus. People with more privilege and comfort must be willing to embrace the vulnerability of recognizing their own need and interdependence on community.

Many church members demonstrate solidarity with each other across life's ups and downs in ways that feel completely instinctive: organizing meal trains for new babies, a death in the family, or an illness; doing a special collection for a family that has lost their home to fire or natural disaster. Crises that are outside the norm evoke our instincts towards mutual aid. But power dynamics of social status, citizenship, class, language, culture, tradition, and ethnicity mean that Christian churches' efforts to give to "the needy" get trapped in paternalistic savior complexes and the desire to control and change those who receive the aid. Combine this with bootstraps individualism, nationalism, the demonization of "handouts," and wealthy power holders' efforts to defund public services to create more profit, and we have a situation in which our natural instincts to share and our Christian call to give to the poor are divorced from their roots in the gospel, corrupted to serve the interests of empire.

Mutual aid calls us not just to share goods and resources, but to dismantle an economic system that relies on there being an underclass in the first place, whose suffering is the human sacrifice upon which wealth is created. Whether or not there is a pandemic or a natural disaster, we are in a constant crisis from an economic system that perpetually exploits poor people's labor, consolidates resources amongst the wealthy, and leaves people sick, hurting, and dying from inequality (see chapter 7). Mutual aid is not about pity—it's about collective salvation. To create common access to resources is to create an interdependent community for mutual flourishing,[11] to create the Kin-dom of God here on Earth as it is in heaven through the sharing of daily bread our Creator provides. When we are engaging in mutual aid as Christians, we are engaging in political commitments for spiritual reasons. Jesus taught us we cannot access God's community if we are hoarding resources that people need to survive.[12] Now is the perfect time for churches to learn from mutual aid networks that exist outside congregational walls in order to better be the church and relearn what, deep down, we already know.

MUTUAL AID IN PRACTICE: THREE STORIES FROM NASHVILLE

Sanctuary Network: When we started to work in mutual aid, we began it as a direct service. We asked church members and allies to join the network by providing resources for community members who lost family members to deportation; these were often women with children who lost the main financial supporter in their homes. Seeing church members willing to support was beautiful. However, we learned that putting someone from the church in relationship with a community member can create unhealthy dependency; by giving power to someone with resources we can cause harm. In one situation, we set up an ambitious system for supporting a family with groceries for nearly a year with donations from congregations, engaging dozens of church volunteers. However, we didn't invest in creating a meaningful path to leadership for the family to become involved in helping others and organizing for change; this created a surface relationship that reinforced powerlessness and dependence instead of what we intended. So, we learned to ask: How are we assuring that impacted people have the power to organize and that strategic conversations are not held unless they are at the table? How do we hold close that access to resources—predominantly money—does not translate into unearned leadership and power? How do we trust that the impacted community's experience makes them the experts?

The Greyhound Network: The MIX was founded on the principle that those from the immigrant community should lead the work to build and protect those same communities. One way the MIX started practicing mutual aid was by participating in the Greyhound Bus mutual aid network, a nationwide grassroots effort to support asylum seekers traveling for days on Greyhound buses with children and little to no supplies, food, or medicine. We volunteered alongside many different people. For many, showing up to support at the bus stations was an eye-opening experience into who asylum seekers were, how they arrived, and what that journey meant to them. But for those from immigrant backgrounds, the asylum seekers' journeys were a trauma-tizing reminder of our own families' experiences: we were remem-bering where we came from, the journey our parents took into the unknown, into a world that already considered you as lesser. We also saw the resilience, the joy, the gratitude, and the bravery every family had when they were met along the way. In conversations with them many shared that they were unafraid but also unsure of what to expect in the states. They shared how it felt to encounter people who volun-teered their welcome and protection, who fed and clothed them — these actions reminding them that the God who protected them and kept them safe while crossing through the desert lands, or riding a train or bus, was also in this nation. Their God was still looking over them and protecting them. Their resilience reminded us that the immigrant community's experience and resilience encourage us to do more and include them in every step of the way.

The Pandemic: When the pandemic hit Nashville, we saw the opportunity to empower those who felt powerless in these moments. We began to organize by talking with, listening to, and validating the struggles of members. The Middle TN Undocufund came from these conversations, which identified a point of service that we could do collectively: a mutual aid fund. Immigrant community members contributed and applied to the fund knowing it was about community supporting community rather than charity. Being involved in the process of raising and distributing the funds allowed for members to continue building relationships with people that we have always seen and known. Because we took crucial steps to involve the community, we deepened trust, we strengthened relationships, and we had conversations about mutual aid, health, and economic justice. We empowered members to step into their power and reflect on the ways our homelands view mutual aid as an ancient sacred practice, one through which we build and move collectively because it means the survival of us all.

LESSONS AND LEARNINGS

Through our experiences we learned significant lessons about how to do mutual aid through a gospel lens.

Build authentic relationships in organic ways. There is both danger and great possibility in encounters across radical difference. We experimented with different ways of building relationships among immigrant communities, religious congregations, volunteers, and organizers. Some of these worked better and had more integrity than others. The most mutually dignifying relationships were formed among people who were doing practical work together even if they came from different backgrounds. For example, people worked together across lines of difference to create bus schedules. Immigrant churches worked with non-immigrant churches to provide childcare and shelter for a family recently arrived from the border. Taking action builds relationships. Practical work builds bonds. In contrast, trying to build relationships in more formal, structured settings, such as presentations to churches or Sunday School classes, often left us feeling like we had put family members' trauma on display without reciprocity: without mutual risk-taking, vulnerability, or commitment to action.

"Service" modes of aid can creep in very easily. We are trained to think in terms of top-down charity, as both givers and receivers; even with the best intentions, our instincts will often revert to charity models. Being honest with each other ahead of time about this, we can build explicitly different ways of doing things and constantly reflect along the way to check on how power dynamics are operating. For instance, are assumptions being made about what is needed without people identifying their needs themselves? Are people with more privilege falling into all the leadership roles? Whose leadership is being seen and valued? How is communication happening? Is language itself creating power dynamics through what is considered "professional" speech and everyone else?

Keep the broader context in view with political education. In a mutual aid project, everyone should be engaged in learning and naming how the dominant economic system operates, what the impact is, who benefits, and how to change it. People can get very comfortable with the details of the work itself without remembering the big picture. We learned that you can very easily get groups of church people to make sandwiches for folks being released from border detention centers, but it is much harder to get them to show up to a protest against private prisons that run those detention centers. So, in our volunteer training we included education about how the detention system works and how we can abolish it. We had to remind ourselves: the point is not to get good at making sandwiches for families released from detention. *The point is to have no more immigrants detained.* We needed to build consciousness among our volunteers so that the same folks buying diapers for a mother whose husband was deported would stand by that same mom and follow her when she was leading a march against the sheriff's office to cut the local ICE contract. *And,* we needed to engage the immigrant mother in such a way that she would see herself not just as someone receiving help in a hard time, but as someone who has the capacity and power to be leading that march, to change the conditions that created her family's hardship. Many faith communities are hesitant because it engages them in actions and conversations perceived as "political." But the gospel always calls us into a different way of being human together.

Be changed. When done well, relationships in mutual aid work *will* transform you and others personally. In the first couple years of the Trump administration, with vehemently anti-immigrant narratives in the news, the immigrant community in Nashville felt they were not wanted. Creating connections between families facing detention and deportation, on the one hand, and supportive congregations, on the other, changed that perception: it awakened immigrant folks to the fact that there were Nashvilleans who wanted them to be there. Likewise, these connections enabled members of the non-immigrant faith community to build real relationships with immigrants in their neighborhood, giving them real experience rather than what they saw on TV. On both sides, the material support and encounters created in the process broke stereotypes and built contexts in which folks saw each other as human.

Seeing non-immigrant congregations exemplify solidarity and sanctuary was an example to immigrant community members of the true reflection of God in Christ, a witness to the church as a dynamic body. This included liberal and progressive congregations already engaged in social justice work, but we also witnessed the consciousness shift within more politically mixed and conservative congregations that counted Trump supporters among their members. When we would put out the call for support for families, for diapers, groceries, and medicine, people responded across party lines, blowing past political boundaries to create a more human community. This showed us how, as we stated earlier, our truest instincts are to care for each other. When you are shopping for the right diaper size for someone's toddler, it becomes much harder to believe in demonizing narratives. The personal, practical realities of mutual aid allowed us to see past our oversimplifications of each other, moving from one-dimensional stories to the full dimensionality and complexity of each other's lives.

HOW TO GET STARTED

With a team, reflect on what you know about your congregation's current models of sharing material resources, within and outside of the church. Who participates, makes decisions, and does the work? How do members become involved? Who dictates who needs support and what kind of support is given? Don't be ashamed if things are not as you wish they would be. Identifying our current structures and their dynamics helps us to name them and see how we already are or are not living into a vision of mutual aid that disrupts our society's power structures in line with the challenge of the gospel. We invite you to look at your congregation as well as at the larger community outside church walls with a new lens. Who do you consider your community? Challenge yourself to push past the concept of what you currently perceive as your community to answer the question: "Who is our neighbor?"

With your team, reflect together on your experiences of having needed support, whether it's been money, skills, or something else. Learn about each other's backgrounds by telling each other stories: Tell a story about a time when you relied on someone else for something essential and it felt good, or about a time you relied on help from others and it felt bad or dehumanizing. What was the difference? How can you create the former experience in your mutual aid, not the latter? These kinds of conversations will help you build important relationships and shared values with each other. Write these values down for sharing, making the language easy to understand and put into practice.

Once you have discerned these questions, learn together about different models of mutual aid, paying particular attention to how the organization centers the participation and leadership of people who are on the receiving end of support. The dire circumstances of the pandemic have invigorated interest in mutual aid across the world. Many people are weary of patronizing or ineffective charity models and want to participate in more dignifying and democratic forms of sharing resources. This means there are valuable opportunities to learn from what others are doing, even if their work is not faith-based.[13] Examples include community bail funds, cop and ICE watch groups, food, medicine, and PPE distribution, and home repair ministries. Keep in mind that while you can learn best practices from other models, no context is the same, and it's fine to adjust.

Now you are ready to design and put into place the practical systems that will help you to share resources in a way that is sustainable. Don't forget to build in regular practices of reflection that will help you collectively stay in your values. Even if we use language of mutual aid, it can be easy for dominant power dynamics to creep in, and so it's best to anticipate how you will course correct rather than be surprised. A simple habit of incorporating regular debriefs with participants asking "What's working? What do we want to do differently?" and "What are we learning?" can help you keep growing instead of falling into routines that don't work or miss important lessons along the way.

Remember that this is all a process. Mutual aid doesn't come into existence in one day, one meeting, even one project. But committing to the long-term work of mutual aid and building a mentality of mutual aid in everything we do helps us come to see the world and each other as God made us to be: as beloved community living out "hoy por ti, mañana por mi." Mutual aid calls us to see sharing our resources as an investment in the whole to create long-lasting change.

When we are attuned to the harsh injustice and inhumanity of a world that feels so impossible to change, mutual aid helps us experience what is possible in a practice of radical hope. It allows us to create alternatives within the unjust structures that dominate, ushering forward an inbreaking of God's creation right here, right now.

BIBLE BLUEPRINT: Matthew 14:15–21 and 15:32–39; Mark 6:30–44 and 8:1–9; Luke 9:11–17; John 6:1–13

The story of Jesus feeding the multitudes by encouraging the mutual sharing of resources (however many loaves and fishes there were starting off the potluck) is the only "miracle" told in all four gospels—sometimes more than once! Jesus knew his people were hungry: Rome stole their land and harvests, leading to hunger and malnutrition. Mutual aid—in this case the community ensuring everyone is fed—is one practice Jesus taught to counter Roman oppression of his people, and the fact that this story is told so many times tells us how key this practice was for the community. —*Anne Dunlap*

Notes

1. English: "Today for you, tomorrow for me."

2. Mixed status means family members have different immigration status, for example some undocumented, some with visas or green cards, and/or some who are citizens.

3. See Luke 12:15, Luke 12:33 for Jesus's statements to rich people, and Matthew 6:19–21, Matthew 6:24–25, Matthew 19:23–24, Luke 18:25, and Luke 6:24 for other commentary from Jesus about wealth and material riches.

4. Acts 4:32. See also the story of Ananias and Sapphira in Acts 5:1–5 for a sobering story of the early church movement's treatment of property-holding people who did not give over the full proceeds from the sale of their land for common use.

5. 1 Corinthians 16:1–4; 2 Corinthians 8:1–9:15; Romans 15:14–32. *Ekklesia* is the Greek word for assembly used in the New Testament and is often, though inaccurately, translated to mean "church."

6. See Rowan Williams, "Sacraments of a New Society," in *On Christian Theology* (Malden, MA: Blackwell, 2000), 209–22.

7. Alexander Zaitchik, "Water is Life: This Is Not A Symbolic Action—Indigenous Protesters Occupy Oil Platforms in Radicalized Fight Against Pollution in the Amazon," *The Intercept*, December 27, 2017, https://theintercept.com/2017/12/27/peru-amazon-oil-pollution-indigenous-protest/.

8. United Church of Christ Baptismal Liturgy, Book of Worship.

9. Adeline Belle Hawes, "Charities and Philanthropies in the Roman Empire," *The Classical Weekly* 6, no. 23 (1913): 178–81.

10. See INCITE! Women of Color Against Violence, ed, *The Revolution Will Not Be Funded: Beyond the Non-Profit Industrial Complex* (Durham: Duke University Press, 2017).

11. John 10:10.

12. See Matthew 19:23–26, Mark 10:24–27, Luke 18:24–27.

13. We recommend Mary Zerkel, "How to Create a Mutual Aid Network," , American Friends Service Committee, August 25, 2021, https://www.afsc.org/blogs/news-and-commentary/how-to-create-mutual-aid-network; Dean Spade, "Solidarity Not Charity: Mutual Aid for Mobilization and Survival." Social Text 142 38, no. 1 (2020): 131–51; as well as the websites Big Door Brigade, "Mutual Aid Toolbox," http://bigdoorbrigade.com /mutual-aid-toolbox/ and Mutual Aid Disaster Relief, https://mutualaiddisaster relief.org/. See also the Mutual Aid section in SURJ-Faith's Resource list: https:// bit.ly/PoliticalEdResources.

15

· · ·

RESISTING WHITE NATIONALISM
Antifascism in the Way of Jesus

· · ·

BRITTANY CAINE-CONLEY

We are marching, in complete silence, toward the unite the right white supremacist rally in downtown Charlottesville, Virginia. We, people of faith representing many traditions, have just been prayed up and sent out of First Baptist Church, the historically Black congregation on Main Street. We cover our unknowing anxiety with intense resolve and moral clarity. As we round the corner and gaze upon the recently renamed Emancipation Park, we encounter heavily armed militia men, dressed in camo fatigues and gripping assault rifles. We move toward them.

While arranging ourselves in a single-file line, facing the monstrous Confederate statue, we pray aloud, persisting with our words while young white men in khakis hurl anti-queer and antisemitic insults toward our hearts. We sing and dance and clap and call loudly for justice to roll down in waves. We petition our God to topple the white nationalist parade of sin and evil.

When we first arrived at the park, the fenced-in, whites-only section was fairly empty. But now, as we fill the streets with a joyful noise, white supremacist, neo-Nazi, and white nationalist groups begin to stream down the hill, passing us on their way into their white ethnic party zone. As the angry white mass grows larger, so does the group of counterprotestors in the street. Community members, activists, antifascists, students, and journalists fill the streets to a frenetically bustling capacity.

The white supremacist clans escalate tension and conflict as they shove, batter, and swing their way through the crowd, attempting to reach their chauvinist buddies inside the white safety zone. Police are inside their own barricades, watching and smirking as white nationalists commit violence with impunity. Once they reach their destination, the neo-Nazis and neo-Confederates join forces to shout their slanders: "Jews will not replace us! White lives matter! The South will rise again! Blood and soil! Russia is our friend! Heil Trump!"

As vitriol and violence swell, we discern the necessity to act. A portion of our faith-filled posse moves to a set of steps outside of the park. We intend to block the stairs, using our bodies and our resolve to demonstrate that white nationalists are not welcome. For weeks we trained for this moment. I believe that we shall not be moved.

A white supremacist clan streams toward us with their batons and helmets and shields. I can barely see what's happening; I am facing the opposite direction on the other side of the body barricade. We thought they'd try to come around the end of our line, so I am stationed there, my feet rooted into the concrete. But they don't come around the end of the line. The brazen bullies use their weapons to push into the center of our holy resistance. Before I can even gather my thoughts or my words, our line opens up, and the raging racists stream right through.

Someone in the front of our crew attempts to sing a half-assed version of "This Little Light of Mine" while the fascists shout "Fuck you!" and slander our divine dignity. I do not sing along. I can only stare at this scene of ultimate failure. I am befuddled, embarrassed, and infuriated. Humiliation swarms my mind and my skin. I wait until the last white supremacist moves past us and I unleash my indignation.

"WHAT THE FUCK JUST HAPPENED? Why did you let them through?" I demand. Voices mumble and feet maneuver and eyes migrate. I'm not sure who opened the line or why the white supremacists were allowed to march right through, but my rage is ready to unleash on the culprit. I channel my anger and move into my best self.

"If we're not actually going to blockade the stairs, then why are we here? If you aren't able to hold the discipline, get off the line." Some folks nod in agreement and we rearrange with me and other local clergy and resistors at the front and center.

As I emotionally wrestle with the chagrin of our botched direct action, a small, unassuming group from Industrial Workers of the World (IWW)[1] ask us if we would like some help. Their offer of assistance and grace in the midst of our shame hits me like a wave of steadfast love. The five of them stand in front of us, ready to use their bodies to protect us from further assault.

The brawling white nationalists do not reach us again. They don't even make it to our new friends from the IWW. The crowded streets grow too thick with antifascist bodies for the neo-Nazis to get through. Even as white supremacists throw their flags and their fists and their clubs toward the resistors in the street, they make no ground. *The procession of white hatred is stopped because anti-fascists and anti-racists use their bodies to absorb the violence.* I watch with awe and gratitude as antifa shows me the way of Jesus, absorbing the violence of systemic evil, so that my beloved community can survive. Antifascists shall not be moved.

OUR CONTEXT AND CALL

Radically[2] resisting evil is the way, the truth, and the life of Jesus. The diversity of tactics that we use to confront and eradicate evil are the Body of Christ. We don't all need to be rallying and marching and chanting in the streets, but we must support and work together with those who are. Those who absorb the violence of raging police and murderous white nationalists are doing the work of the resurrected Christ. Jesus the Christ absorbed violence so that others could live and thrive. The wandering carpenter from Nazareth took on the cross of oppression to bring good news to the poor, to proclaim release to the captives, and to let the oppressed go free. The purveyors of brutal authoritarianism and imperial power hung Jesus from a tree. The term fascism wasn't coined until the early twentieth century, but in first-century Palestine, Jesus the Christ rose from his grave and demonstrated antifascism by overcoming the violent nationalism that attempted to take his life.

When the alt-right displayed vicious hatred in Charlottesville in August of 2017, it was radical antifascists (antifa), antiracists, and community defenders who absorbed that violence and prevented more from taking place. Police consistently agitated and persecuted activists and Black and Brown folks in Charlottesville, and then allowed white nationalists to do the same. I've found that this cycle, in which police protect white supremacists (or white property) while doing significant harm to Black and brown folks, is true in every community.

Courageous folks in Ferguson showed us how to resist a violent police state. In Charlottesville, we had to learn how to resist violent white militias and neo-Nazis who were aided and abetted by militarized police and willfully obtuse systems of government (and religion). More recently, during the January 2021 white supremacist insurrection in Washington, DC, we witnessed police officers move barriers and fences so the white horde could advance, while others posed for selfies with those who had the Capitol under siege. Many political leaders encouraged the violence or kept silent in order to protect their reelection chances.

Throughout the spring and summer of 2017, antifascist activists provided information to Charlottesville city officials about the violent intentions of those planning and attending the Unite the Right rally. The local police, city government, and many church leaders ignored the pleas of activists and encouraged the community to stay home and allow white violent nationalists to have their ethnic cleansing celebration in our progressive civil town. Antifascists knew what to expect because they have been tracking and confronting fascism in all its forms for many years, but they were ignored, criminalized, and scapegoated. By discounting antifascists and branding antiracist activists as violent and extreme, the official powerbrokers in Charlottesville created a safe space for bloodthirsty fascism.

After the mobs of white nationalists brutalized my community, I was devastated to hear a "both sides" narrative unfolding. White terrorists assaulted my friends, and the forty-fifth president declared there were very fine people on "both sides." Many computer screen commentators blamed the violence on those of us who took to the streets to resist white supremacy. The alt-right placed me on a list of "antifa leaders." When a seemingly well-intentioned relative exclaimed, "Those antifa guys sure are scary!" I was stunned. I told her, "Antifa saved my life."

Amid rapidly escalating civil unrest, those in positions of power and privilege often convince us that radicals are destroying our decorum and democracy. We desire peace without justice. We worship civility. We call for nonviolence without challenging the violence done by our systems, our privilege, our inaction, and our silence. We blame conflict on those who tear down the illusions of democracy that kept us comfortable. We use religious dogma and religious power to stay far away from conflict. We convince ourselves that we are creating God's kin-dom with our book studies and our prayer breakfasts and our charity bake sales.

Hear this: Our civility will not save us. Our civility will not allow justice to roll down like waters, or righteousness like an ever-flowing stream. Our proliferation of conflict-free "peace" will codify a status quo that harms those who are already suffering. Our criminalization of those who radically confront evil will embolden, empower, and unleash the very real forces of violent white supremacy that plague our communities.

Our current reality is that evil white fascist clans are propped up by murderous militarized police and the deliberately debilitating decorum of institutional power. As followers of Jesus the Christ, who challenged evil power and overcame death, we must radically resist the violence of nationalism and white supremacy culture. We must lean into our discomfort to support those who are doing the work of absorbing violence and confronting brutality. We must form new coalitions between antifa and clergy, anarchists and church ladies.

Don't allow sensationalized news cycles to scare you. Every apostle of justice has been declared too radical. Jesus was executed for acts of sedition. Rev. Dr. Martin Luther King, Jr. was labeled a communist and stalked by the CIA. The FBI constantly surveilled the black poets, authors, and activists that we now celebrate. Alicia Garza, Opal Tometi, and Patrisse Khan-Cullors, the women who ignited the Black Lives Matter movement, have been called terrorists and have been harassed consistently by white nationalists and by those who simply call themselves "conservative." So many white Christians want to quote the late great congressman and activist John Lewis and call for "good trouble," and yet the majority of these online advocates are unwilling to support activists who are actually being persecuted by the state for acts of subversive and revolutionary justice. We must challenge ourselves to follow those who are considered too radical and unruly.

WHAT CAN CHURCHES DO?

Church folks will often cringe at the thought of supporting and collaborating with radical activists. In Charlottesville, I received consistent pushback from church folks who were uncomfortable with a "fuck white supremacy" sign, who were opposed to activists yelling in the streets, who believed being peaceful meant being silent and passive. Some of those church folks were able to lean into their discomfort and experience beloved community. *Being able to join together with anarchist activists, queer Rabbis, black mamas, transgender teenagers, old church ladies, and Muslim students to share a meal together before marching in the streets for justice was the most sacred and holy work I've ever done.* It was truly a vision of God's reign. However, most church folks did not come alongside our multifaceted movement for liberation. And that's OKAY. It's unlikely you will get your entire congregation to show up in new and difficult ways. Find those who are able to dream and question and reimagine and put your focus there.

There are people in your geographical community already doing the work of antiracism and antifascism. Some of them are organizing systems of mutual aid for sharing resources and building solidarity. Some are creating networks of community defense, so that marginalized peoples don't need to rely on the police. And yes, some antiracists and antifascists are out in the street, loudly demanding justice and confronting evil head on. Here are some ways you can get connected and begin to forge transformational partnerships:

Research mutual aid in your community. Mutual aid is about building community-level structures of cooperation and solidarity, instead of the distant charity model where those with resources give a little of their abundance to those in need. This often includes distributing groceries and medicine, providing survival supplies, or redistributing other resources. Join a mutual aid network or ask those providing mutual aid how you can get involved (see chapter 14).

Attend a non-violent direct-action training. If you can't find any happening in your community, contact groups or organizations hosting trainings in other cities and ask them for recommendations in your area. Those doing the work of antiracism and antifascism are well connected nationally. You definitely have six or less degrees of separation to a radical activist somewhere! (See chapter 4).

Find bail support or court support groups near you. These groups are working to provide care and resources to people being harmed by an unjust criminal justice system. Ask how you can contribute and send money their way.

Start showing up and take a buddy. Show up to a rally, protest, vigil, march, or other events hosted by groups in your area. Listen and learn and get to know the people there. Some suggestions for groups to follow include Black Lives Matter (BLM), Showing Up for Racial Justice (SURJ), and Democratic Socialists of America (DSA). There are many other local groups who do this work and groups vary in terms of ideology and tactics. You can use your judgement in deciding who to support but remember to challenge your privileged ideas of civility and peace and politics.

THINGS TO REMEMBER

Dispel the myth of the "good protestor." Protestors are always despised by those in power, no matter their tactics. The purpose of protest is to disrupt business as usual. If an action is not disruptive or discomforting, it's not a protest.

White nationalist groups are a serious threat everywhere. Do your own research by checking out the Southern Poverty Law Center (https://www.splcenter.org/).

Coalition building to confront and resist white supremacist fascism is really hard work. You will encounter disagreement and conflict and your feelings will get hurt (more than once). Practice grace-filled accountability. Apologize when you mess up. Share food and laughter together. It's worth it. We need all of us.

There is space for everyone in movement work. In Charlottesville, we created a large web of support (infrastructure) for our actions. The world saw pictures of us marching in the street, but we wouldn't have been there without a multitude of so many folks doing work behind the scenes.

- A church opened its doors to be a safe haven for protestors and community members, providing space for mental health care, first aid, snacks, and water (no cops or alt-right allowed). The SURJ-Faith Community Safety Toolkit has helpful resources on how to create a safe space without police (see chapter 12).[3]

- Different teams handled communication and press, making sure everyone on the ground got updated information. Press training was provided for those who would be giving statements and talking with reporters.

- Street medics provided immediate care to those who were harmed. Street medic training was held the months leading up to the rally. Care Bears, volunteers with backpacks full of supplies, were organized to take food, water, and safety supplies to those in the street.

- Another church set up an aftercare location for protestors who might be arrested. A bail team was prepared to bail protestors out of jail and engage with the magistrate. Once at the church, protesters would receive food, water, clothing, and mental health care. After a white supremacist attacked protestors with his car, clergy and congregants from the church were dispatched to the hospital to provide support for those who were attacked (see chapter 4).

- A local restaurant provided a safe space for our group to rest and recharge during a day filled with conflict and trauma. The restaurant owner fed us and hired a security team to keep us safe.

- Trauma care providers provided free and discounted resources for ongoing care of the community. Those who needed care were able to receive therapy, yoga sessions, massage, and other lifesaving services.

The violence we experienced in Charlottesville was not an anomaly. White nationalist groups continue to escalate violence across our country and across the globe. From Portland to Denver to Kenosha to Detroit to DC, violent white nationalists are planning and executing unconscionable brutality. In January of 2021, many white neoliberal and progressive Americans were surprised and appalled by the white nationalist insurrection at the Capitol. Those who have long been doing the work of resisting white supremacy were not surprised. While we continue to wish for a change in the rhetoric coming from our political leaders, we must acknowledge that white supremacist groups will do everything in their power to organize and brutalize, no matter who sits in the halls of power. Our systems of governance are deeply rooted in white supremacy and our bipartisan politicking will not bring about the antiracist, antifascist future that we desire.

Our call is urgent and it is clear: "We who believe in freedom cannot rest."[4] We who believe in freedom must radically resist violent white nationalism. Let us be antifascist, let us be antiracist, and let it be so.

BIBLE BLUEPRINT: James 2:8–9, 14

Love is without hierarchy or borders. Love doesn't assign rank or value based on difference. Love does not seek to be exalted at the detriment of any part of creation. Love is radical because in its purest essence, love enfolds, covers, and welcomes rather than repels, devalues, and violates. May we embody the love that dwells in us and face evil, together. May we perpetually return to love's well as we reject evil in its vile forms of oppression and dehumanizing expressions, ideals, and systems. May we press forward together, tapping into the source and substance of our resolve, love. —*Vahisha Hasan*

Notes

1. The Industrial Workers of the World is a global union dedicated to direct action, solidarity, and industrial democracy.

2. Our word *radical* was formed from the Latin adjective *radicalis*, which simply meant "of or relating to a root." The Latin word *radix* meant "root." So when we say radical, we don't just mean unusual or intense. When we are radical, we are rooted, grounded, and getting to the heart of the matter.

3. "Invitation to Prophetic Imagination: Community Safety for All: Congregational Action Toolkit a Project of SURJ-Faith," *Showing Up for Racial Justice–SURJ*, https://surj.org/our-work/surj-faith/cs4a/.

4. Sweet Honey in the Rock, "Ella's Song," *Breaths*, 1988. "Ella's Song" is dedicated to civil rights leader Ella Baker, who said, "Until the killing of black men, black mothers' sons, becomes as important to the rest of the country as the killing of a white mother's son, we who believe in freedom cannot rest until this happens."

· · ·

LIST OF ORGANIZATIONS
NAMED IN CHAPTERS
(and others you might find helpful!)

· · ·

ACLU Ohio
https://www.acluohio.org

Act Up
https://actupny.com/ (current)
https://actupny.org/documents/Marshall.html
(archive, Marshall resources)

A Just Harvest
https://ajustharvest.org/

American Disabled For Attendant Programs Today (ADAPT)
https://adapt.org

American Indian Movement of Colorado
https://colorado-aim.blogspot.com

Appalshop
https://appalshop.org

Arts and Democracy
https://artsanddemocracy.org

Beautiful Trouble Toolbox
https://www.beautifultrouble.org

Big Door Brigade (Mutual Aid)
http://bigdoorbrigade.com

Black Church Food Security Network
https://blackchurchfoodsecurity.net

Black Liturgies
https://colearthurriley.com

Black Lives Matter Global Network (BLM)
https://blacklivesmatter.com

The BlackOut Collective
https://blackoutcollective.org

Causa Justa
https://cjjc.org

The Catalyst Project
https://collectiveliberation.org

Children's Defense Fund
https://www.childrensdefense.org

Church World Service
https://cwsglobal.org/our-work/north-america/advocacy-and-organizing

Critical Resistance
http://criticalresistance.org

Democratic Socialists of America
https://www.dsausa.org

Detention Watch Network
https://www.detentionwatchnetwork.org

Do No Harm Coalition
https://www.donoharmcoalition.org

Enfleshed
https://enfleshed.com

Faith For Justice
https://www.faithforjustice.org

Faith Matters Network Movement Chaplaincy Project
https://www.faithmattersnetwork.org/daringcompassion

Forward Justice
https://forwardjustice.org

Four Winds American Indian Council
https://www.fourwindscenter.org

The Gamaliel Network
https://gamaliel.org

generative somatics
https://generativesomatics.org

Girl Trek
http://girltrek.org

The Highlander Center
https://highlandercenter.org

Industrial Workers of the World
https://iww.org

Interfaith Immigration Coalition
https://www.interfaithimmigration.org

Law for Black Lives
http://www.law4blacklives.org

Live Free USA
http://www.livefreeusa.org

Many Voices: A Black Church Movement for Gay and
Transgender Justice
https://www.manyvoices.org

Melekte Melaku:
https://www.acluohio.org/en/biographies/melekte-melaku

MICAH: Memphis Interfaith Coalition for Action and Hope
https://www.micahmemphis.org

Movement for Black Lives (M4BL)
https://m4bl.org

Mutual Aid Disaster Relief:
https://mutualaiddisasterrelief.org

Netroots Nation: Digital Tactics for Direct Action
https://www.netrootsnation.org/nn_events/nn20/digital-tactics-for-
direct-action

Poor People's Campaign
https://www.poorpeoplescampaign.org

Project South
https://projectsouth.org

Restoration Village Arts
https://restorationvillagearts.org

The Rev. James Lawson Institute
https://jameslawsoninstitute.org

Samuel DeWitt Proctor Conference
https://sdpconference.info

Sanctuary Not Deportation (including Interfaith Sanctuary Toolkit)
http://sanctuarynotdeportation.org

School of the Americas Watch
https://soaw.org

Showing Up for Racial Justice (SURJ)
https://surj.org

Soulforce
https://www.soulforce.org

Southern Crossroads
https://www.fight4thesouth.org

Southern Poverty Law Center (SPLC)
https://www.splcenter.org

Southerners on New Ground (Song)
https://southernersonnewground.org

Trauma Response and Crisis Care for Movement (TRACC)
https://www.tracc4movements.com

United Church of Christ Immigration Resources
https://www.ucc.org/justice_immigration

United Church of Christ Join the Movement for Racial Justice
https://jointhemovementucc.org

Veterans of Hope
https://www.veteransofhope.org

. . .

CONTRIBUTORS

. . .

Rev. Anne Dunlap is the Faith Organizing Coordinator for Showing Up for Racial Justice (SURJ), a UCC minister, and the founder of FierceRev Remedies. Nurtured into faith-rooted organizing in the Central America solidarity movement in the 1980s, she is grateful to Central American, Black, immigrant, worker, and indigenous leaders who have challenged her to think and act deeply about what it means to be human, and to be free. Proud to be from Arkansas, Anne now lives in Buffalo, NY, with her beloved and their kitty.

Rev. Ayanna Johnson Watkins (she/her) is a clergyperson and community organizer focused on building transformative community and nurturing the God-given purpose of each individual. She earned her BA in sociology from Yale University and both her MDiv and MA in social service administration from the University of Chicago—then stayed in Chicago for another ten years working as a writer, social worker, pastor, teacher, and community organizer. Ayanna now lives with her husband and two daughters in Memphis, TN, where she is honored to be lead organizer and executive director of Memphis Interfaith Coalition for Action & Hope (MICAH).

Cathy Carrillo is an immigrant rights advocate and community organizer in Nashville, TN and has been at the forefront of local movements to end immigrant detention. Cathy served as the community defense organizer for Southeast Immigrant Rights Network, and is the co-founder of the MIX, a young adult activist group that has organized in response to ICE raids and detentions in the Nashville community. Cathy has been integral in the planning of the Women's March in Nashville. In addition to her role as a leader in community organizing spaces, Cathy is also a trained birth doula and newborn care specialist.

Rev. Dr. Chris S. Davies grew up in Connecticut, lives in Cleveland, and is a wandering Irish Rover at heart. She is grounded in community and continuing to learn in faith and live justly, serving Christ in all things. Chris is a queer femme, an urban farmer and beekeeper, and a creative networker of communities. She is passionate about justice and Jesus, and organizes with Showing Up For Racial Justice in Northeast Ohio.

Erica N. Williams, MDiv (she/her) is a spiritual leader and international human rights activist. Currently, she is a student in the inaugural cohort for the master's in religion and public life program at Harvard Divinity School. Erica is the founding pastor of Set It Off Ministries and a national social justice organizer for Repairers of the Breach and the Poor People's Campaign: A National Call for Moral Revival. Williams is a member of the Freedom Church of the Poor, Popular Education Project, Black Christians for Palestine, and a Trustee for the World Student Christian Federation. She is ordained in the Christian Church (Disciples of Christ). Her life's mission is summed up in the social gospel passage of Luke 4:18–19. She is a native of Saginaw, MI.

Jade T. Perry, MEd (she/her) is a writer, speaker, educator, artist, and mystic. She is a BlackQueerDisabledFemme practicing contemplative and spiritual activism. As a co-founder of the Mystic Soul Project (501c3 nonprofit organization), she works to center people of color in healing, mysticism, and activism. Jade has extensive training in integrative and interdisciplinary Arts and over seven years of experience in social justice and higher education. She mixes these disciplines in order to provide training, project and org consultation, and workshop facilitation on a variety of topics. Jade carries on the tradition of folk healing in new ways, attempting to expand upon and reinterpret the gifts given by her foremothers. She is attuned to Reiki Level II and developed the intuitive gift of clairvoyance in the Black supernaturalist church. Now as a multi-faithed, sex-positive, Black Feminist spiritual advisor and folk-healer, you can find her discussing POC-centered wellness, art-as-ritual, or providing individual tarot reading or energy healing sessions. The mission of her work, as a whole, is to contribute resources, art, narratives, and experiential learning opportunities that aid in the holistic healing processes of Blackfolk, Queer and Trans Black and Indigenous People of Color (QTBIPOC), and disabled and/or chronically ill folks within these communities.

Logan Rimel is a denominationally polyamorous church nerd seeking after that God who breaks unjust barriers and blends binaries. They currently attend Pacific Lutheran Theological Seminary in Berkeley, CA, and are a camp counselor and co-director at The Naming Project, a Christian summer camp for youth of all sexual orientations and gender identities.

Rev. Lucy Waechter Webb (she/her) is a politicized faith leader ordained in the Presbyterian Church (USA). After ten years in parish ministry, her ministry is now focused on engaging other racialized white people in antiracism practice, as she is always deepening her own. She resides on unceded Anishinaabek territory otherwise known as Leelanau County, MI. Her children are some of her best teachers, as are the trees and garden.

Rev. Margaret Ernst was born in New England on traditional Wampanoag land and has been organizing faith communities for justice since 2013, including with POWER (Philadelphians Organized to Witness, Empower and Rebuild), Showing Up for Racial Justice, and Faith Matters Network. From 2016 to 2018, she built a network of congregations working in solidarity with people facing deportation in middle Tennessee. Margaret completed her master of divinity at Vanderbilt Divinity School and is ordained in the United Church of Christ.

Rev. Dr. Marilyn Pagán-Banks (she/her/ella) is a queer womanist minister, healer, writer, and life-long co-learner committed to the liberation of oppressed and colonized peoples, building power, and creating community. She currently serves as executive director of A Just Harvest, pastor at San Lucas UCC, and adjunct professor at McCormick Theological Seminary. Rev. Pagán-Banks received her master of divinity from McCormick Theological Seminary and her doctorate in ministry from the Chicago Theological Seminary, where she was twice named Hispanic Scholar. She is a joyful contributor in the book *Words of Her Mouth: Psalms for the Struggle*. Rev. Pagán-Banks lives in Chicago with her spouse and loves laughing and dancing with her beautiful grandchildren.

Nichola Torbett is a spiritual seeker, recovering addict, gospel preacher, podcaster, writer, resistance fomenter, dog-walker, nonviolent direct action trainer, and aspiring race traitor. Driven by her passion for both spiritual formation and social change, she co-founded Seminary of the Street, a training academy for love warriors, in 2009, and Second Acts, a liturgical direct action affinity group, in 2014. She is co-editor of *Resipiscence: A Lenten Devotional for Dismantling White Supremacy* and a frequent contributor to "The Word Is Resistance," a podcast from SURJ-Faith, *enfleshed*, and GEEZ magazine.

Rev. Noel Andersen is the director of grassroots organizing for Church World Service, where he has developed a national network of faith communities taking action in solidarity with immigrants and refugees. He is ordained in the United Church of Christ (UCC) and is the lead organizer and cofounder of the UCC National Collaborative on Immigration, a grassroots network of UCC leaders taking action for immigrants' rights. He has worked for a number of nonprofit organizations in Central America and on the US–Mexico border focusing on community development, education, and community organizing. Noel works to engage faith communities in the growing Sanctuary Movement's prophetic resistance to deportation policies. He was instrumental in creating a Refugee Leadership Development for Social Change project at CWS, helping to train hundreds of refugees in community organizing. Noel has been quoted in numerous media outlets including the *New York Times*, *Los Angeles Times*, Reuters, and the *Washington Post*. He was recently honored with an award from the National Council of Churches for Excellence in Faithful Leadership.

Rev. Sandra Summers is a Christian pastor's kid who attempted to stay in college forever before entering ministry. After serving the local church, Sandra is now a spiritual coach for children and adults. Her call focuses on helping individuals stay in love with their ministry. Sandra is ordained in the UCC with standing in the DOC. She currently lives in Memphis, TN with her husband, Rev. Sam Teitel, her son Gideon, and their rescue dog Tommy.

Rev. Sèkinah Hamlin is a mother, caregiver, pastor, and the minister for economic justice for the United Church of Christ. Her ministry helps to re-create this world into one that is just for all—a world rooted in biblical principles of jubilee and the life of Jesus Christ.

Sky Roosevelt-Morris belongs to the White Mountain N'dee Nation and the Shawnee Nation. She is on the leadership council of the American Indian Movement of Colorado, council member on Four Winds American Indian Council, member of Tall Bull Memorial Council, and scholar at the Fourth World Center for the Study of Indigenous Law and Politics housed in the political science department at the University of Colorado Denver.

Rev. Smash (Brittany Caine-Conley) is a pastor, teacher, and organizer who was baptized by antiracist fire while resisting and counteracting white supremacist violence in Charlottesville, VA. She is rooted in the subversive way of Jesus and enjoys dancing, deconstructing destructive dominions of dominance, and alliterations. Smash is ordained in the United Church of Christ and seeks beloved community wherever she goes.

Rev. Tracy Howe is a cultural worker, integrating songwriting, music production, and liturgy into organizing, community building, and healing. She serves as the Minister for Congregational and Community Engagement for the UCC National Setting working intersectionally and creatively to address complex realities in the church and world towards a just world for all. She is the founder of Restoration Village Arts and is pursuing a PhD in applied intercultural arts research at the University of Arizona.

Rev. Vahisha Hasan, the Executive Director of Movement in Faith, is deeply invested in ways activist and faith communities further collective healing and liberation. She is also board chair of Transform Network, the rapid response coordinator for TRACC4Movements

(Trauma Response and Crisis Care) and program director at the Historic Clayborn Temple in Memphis TN. Vahisha is her best self in beloved community and deeply grateful for her biological, chosen, and movement family. You can find her moving to the end of her own rainbow in the US South and on IG and Twitter @VHasanMIF. .

Rev. Dr. Velda Love currently serves as Minister for Racial Justice in the Justice and Local Church Ministries of the United Church of Christ National Office in Cleveland, OH, developing opportunities to engage in antiracism trainings, workshops, and critical race education. Velda also develops resources in an effort to equip UCC congregations to be on a restorative racial justice journey in order to dismantle and eradicate structural, systemic, and individual racism. "Racism is a philosophy based on contempt for life. It is the arrogant assertion that one race is the center of value and object of devotion, before which other races must kneel in submission." (MLK, Jr.) God is the Creator of humanity and does not place one group of people above another.

Teresa Mateus is an author, speaker, trauma specialist, educator, and mystic. She is the executive director and co-founder of the Mystic Soul Project and co-founder and program coordinator for TRACC (trauma response and crisis care) 4 Movements. She is a graduate of NYU School of Clinical Social Work and Sivananda Yoga Teacher Training, and is a student of Indigenous healing within the Incan Lineage of Q'ero Paqos as well as BIPOC-centered herbalism. Teresa has provided individual, community, and organizational support and consultation at the intersections of healing, spirituality, and activism, prioritizing BIPOC/QTPOC centering space-creation. Teresa is the author of three books: *Sacred Wounds: A Path to Healing from Spiritual Trauma*, *Mending Broken: A Personal Journey Through the Stages of Trauma + Recovery*, and *Going Naked: The Camino de Santiago & Life as Pilgrimage*.